THE STORY OF THE WORLD'S FAVOURITE MODEL RACING CARS

HarperCollins*Illustrated*

THE STORY OF THE WORLD'S FAVOURITE MODEL RACING CARS

ROD GREEN

HarperCollins*Illustrated*

Acknowledgements

Special thanks are due to collector Chris Gregory (chris_gregory@hotmail.com),
Simon Kohler at Scalextric and Susan Pownall of *Racer* magazine.

First published in Great Britain in 2001 by HarperCollins

an imprint of HarperCollins*Publishers*

77–85 Fulham Palace Road

London W6 8JB

www.**fire**and**water**.com

Designed, edited and created by Essential Books

The right of Rod Green to be identified as the author of this work has been asserted by him
in accordance with the Copyright, Designs and Patents Act 1988

10 9 8 7 6 5 4 3 2 1

Printed in Great Britain by Bath Press

A catalogue record for this book is available from the British Library

ISBN 0-00-713421-5

Introduction

Above The start banner fitted, unsurprisingly, over the starting grid

Right Staggered start positions helped to take away the advantage held by the car on the inside lane when it came to the first corner

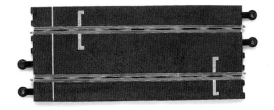

Scalextric's 1995 catalogue claimed that 'Scalextric can be all things to all men.' I can think of quite a few things it will never be for me, but what it most certainly *will* always be is fun.

In a way, though, the catalogue had a point. Scalextric has become more than just a toy. It is an all-consuming hobby for many dedicated racers – some might say it's even a competitive sport. For others it is a business. Buying, selling and collecting models and paraphernalia can be a real money-spinner. All the same, you can never get away from fact number one – that Scalextric was always intended and is still intended to be a fun thing to race.

I suppose it's a childhood memory trick – it always snowed at Christmas, it was always warm and sunny in the summer, and Scalextric was always fun. There were never any problems when I was a kid with cars overheating, fiddly little electrical pick-ups that were almost impossible to replace, track connections that wouldn't connect, or banking on curves that collapsed if you even breathed near them . . . were there? No, Scalextric was always hugely entertaining, always unbearably exciting,

always fantastic fun. It was the toy that every dad could share with his son, the one that came top of the Christmas list for every boy. And girls? Well, they came later.

For any of us hovering around the forty-year mark who grew up in the Sixties, such was our indoctrination with the name (although most of us pronounced it wrongly – Scalectrix instead of Scalextric) that it became a generic term. Scalextric was to slot-car racing like Coke was to cola and Hoover was to vacuum cleaners. You had to feel sorry for any kid who was given a racing set that wasn't Scalextric. 'Accept no substitute' might as well have been the motto of the day.

Scalextric weren't slow to pick up on the brand loyalty generated by their product and from the early Sixties they encouraged their young (and not so young) clients to form their own racing

Right Scalextric was manufactured in France, Spain, Hong Kong, Mexico and the Soviet Union. These are Spanish catalogue covers

clubs and join the Scalextric Association. The official enthusiasts' organisation has changed in shape and form many times over the years and is now stronger than ever. The Scalextric Enthusiasts Club has members all over the world and produces a regular magazine called *Racer* to keep everyone up to date not only with the latest product lines but also with the racing competitions organised by the international network of different clubs, and real motor-sport events. It also informs its readers of the whereabouts of the Scalextric Roadshow.

Hints and tips on how to improve your circuit or your racing technique are also featured, but the Enthusiasts Club doesn't only exist on the printed page, it gets involved with its members. They helped 1999 Junior Scalextric Champion Ben Harding make it into the record books when he raced a car around the world's longest track – 2,550 feet – during the making of a new Scalextric video.

Special limited-edition cars are also made available to club members via *Racer* magazine and

collectors belonging to the NSCC. This collectors' club has now been around for over twenty years and is in fact international, with a membership of over 1,000 worldwide. The 200th edition of the NSCC newsletter was celebrated with a special-edition green Jaguar XJ220 decorated with a gold NSCC emblem on the bonnet. Special cars have also been produced for certain retailers such as Toys 'R' Us and Beatties.

Some cars, of course, are sought out by collectors for their rarity value. Models produced in France and Spain, for example, were manufactured in colours never available in the UK. Indeed, some cars themselves were never officially available in the UK, with cars like the Renault 12 Gordini obviously having a far greater appeal in France than they would anywhere else. In the Seventies, Scalextric was even produced under licence in the Soviet Union, where the sets they manufactured contained the Ford-Mirage and Lamborghini Miura models. The Russian versions turned out to be

Left The Le Mans Bentley is a Scalextric collector's favourite. The one on the left has been lovingly chrome plated

of inferior quality, and the sneaky Soviet practice of exporting them back into the UK had to be swiftly snuffed out.

There were plenty of home-grown anomalies too. Some cars that appeared in the UK catalogue never actually made it into production – two prime examples are the Ford Sierra XR4i and Lancia Delta. It's a problem inherent in the production of a catalogue that elements of it will be out of date almost the moment the ink hits the paper. Some models will be latecomers that miss one catalogue, appearing in the next as new cars for that year even though they've been out there in the marketplace for most of the preceding year. Other cars might fall foul of manufacturing glitches and not appear in the shops at all that season. Many catalogue entries will be prototypes that will undergo detail changes prior to production.

Trying to keep the range as contemporary as possible has also always had its problems. In the old days, designing and tooling up for the manufacture of a Scalextric model could take up to 18 months, though modern production processes have drastically reduced that time. So keeping up with the changing face of motor racing occasionally called for a gamble. The six-wheeled March Ford of 1978 looked great in Scalextric form, but no one could have predicted that it would be deemed such a turkey by March that it would never be raced in anger. The six-wheeled Tyrrell, on the other hand, saw significant racing success, but the model was produced in Spain and never appeared in a UK catalogue.

The vast scale of the Scalextric operation over the years has produced enough rare and valuable cars to hold the interest of collectors and dealers for years to come, but this book aims chiefly to take a nostalgic look at the mainstream of over forty years of Scalextric history. Some of the older cars will certainly bring back memories for some of us older Scalextric fans, and the details about the cars on which they were based are intended to explain why certain cars were chosen to join the range by reviewing some key events in motor sport. Comparing the older cars and accessories with the newer ones will also show how Scalextric, which many point out has changed so little over the past four decades that today's cars can still race on the original track and vice versa, has actually changed quite a bit. Try racing a Protec Audi A4 against a tin-plate Maserati 250F and see which one corners closer, accelerates faster, hugs the track better and crosses the finishing line first. The on-screen computer scoreboard will let you know who's doing best during the race.

Now firmly embracing the microchip age, Scalextric models are produced using computer-aided design technology and raced on circuits that can incorporate more high-tech gadgets than the bridge of the starship *Enterprise*. And, naturally, Scalextric has its own website. If you try searching the web for Scalextric in the UK and Eire, you will score more than 3,600 hits. Most of these are for dealers, retailers, collectors, racing clubs and mad-keen enthusiasts. Scalextric's site is at www.scalextric.com, or you can log on to Scalextric USA at www.scalextric-usa.com.

Don't go rushing off to your PC without having read this book first, though. There's still a lot of fun to be had with old-fashioned print media. There's that word again – 'fun'. There's a chance that it may get slightly over-used in the following pages, but I make no apologies for that.

Fun, after all, is what Scalextric is all about.

As with real Racing Cars your Scalextric Car may from time to time require servicing. Official Scalextric Service Dealers have been appointed throughout the country and they are fully equipped and qualified to effect rapid servicing and repairs to all Scalextric Equipment. Scalextric Service Dealers also carry a comprehensive range of Spares for those enthusiasts who wish to carry out their own servicing.

Scalextric approved Service Dealers are provided with this window Display Badge.

SCALEXTRIC

OFFICIAL SERVICE DEALER

This catalogue illustrates and refers to a number of items which are the subjects of Patent and Registered Designs in Great Britain and many other important countries throughout the world. Details of these are available from Minimodels Ltd., Havant, Hants.

Minimodels Ltd., reserve the right to alter designs and specifications without prior notice. This catalogue supersedes all previous editions.

MINIMODELS LTD.
HAVANT HANTS
ENGLAND

THE THRILL OF **SCALEXTRIC** MOTOR RACING by

WORLD CHAMPION DRIVER

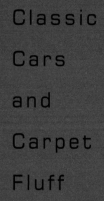

Classic

Cars

and

Carpet

Fluff

Classic Cars and Carpet Fluff

How exciting is it to be eight or nine years old? Every day there's something new to do, something you discover, something so fantastically brilliant that only wriggling about, shouting really loud, jumping up and down and running around can stop that wriggly, shouty, jumpy, running-around feeling from making you swell up like a gigantic balloon till you're ready to burst.

If you were eight or nine in 1957, that wriggly, shouty, jumpy, run-around feeling may now be just a grainy old black and white memory, although it could well be fortified by watching your grandchildren performing the same antics. Any parent or grandparent nowadays will be perfectly familiar with the catalyst that sets off the wriggly-shouty-jumpies because they're the ones who end up coughing up for the latest computer game, DVD, CD or toy. So what was it that flipped the uncontainable excitement switch for a child in 1957?

In Britain, rationing of food, clothes and other goods harking back to the dark days of World War II had ended three years previously and the country was galloping towards the boom years of the Sixties. Over half the homes in Britain had a television set, and there were great groans of anguish when the television licence fee went up from £1 to £4. TV detector vans were introduced that year to catch those who were tuning in without paying up! There were only two channels available, BBC and the new ITV, which had now been broadcasting for two years. Children were watching *The Woodentops*, *Captain Pugwash* and *The Flowerpot Men* or sophisticated American imported series like *Champion the Wonderhorse*, *Hawkeye and the Last of the Mohicans* or *The Lone Ranger*.

The biggest-selling toy of the year was the hula hoop, while in America, where Elvis had just moved into his Gracelands mansion, there was a brand-new invention – the frisbee. The most exciting thing of all, however, happened early in the year when the last page of the *Beano* annual from Christmas had barely been read for the tenth or twentieth time. At the annual Toy Fair in Harrogate, a new toy was launched – Scalextric.

The brainchild of Mr B F Francis, the proprietor

Right Sunbeam Alpine Startex and MG TF Scalex bearing the battle scars of half a century's play

of a company called Minimodels, Scalextric was developed from his Scalex model car range. These tin-plate toys had been introduced in 1952 and were modelled on some of the most glamorous sports racing cars of the time, starting with the Jaguar XK120.

The 1:32 scale XK120 model was a beautifully executed rendition of the car that had made Jaguar an international success. The real XK120 had been unveiled at the London Motor Show in 1948 and was an instant hit both as a road car and a racing car. The styling caused a sensation, although some remained sceptical that it could actually achieve its purported top speed of 120 mph (XK was the engine designation and 120 the claimed speed). The sceptics were silenced when, before any customers had received production models, the new Jaguar was driven along a stretch of Belgian motorway in front of the world's media at speeds of over 130 mph.

In its first outing at a race meeting at Silverstone in 1949, the UK's first postwar production car race,

Above Underside of the MG TF Scalex model showing the fifth 'winding' wheel

Left Jaguar's XK120, the car on which the very first Scalex model was based

the XK120 won hands down. The following year the car was to win the gruelling Alpine Trial in France at the hands of rally aces Ian and Patricia Appleyard, and in America Leslie Johnson competed in the Sports Car Club of America road race at Palm Beach Shores in Florida, winning the Healey Trophy for 'best production car'.

The Scalex XK120 couldn't quite match the performance of its bigger brother, but it did have a few unique performance tricks of its own. Its clockwork motor was wound not by a key but by a cunning 'fifth wheel' device. The extra wheel was hidden underneath the car just behind the front axle and when the car was pressed down on a hard surface and pulled backwards, the wheel wound up the clockwork motor. Release the car and away it went. Not too good on a thick carpet, but on 1950s lino it was a winner!

The Scalex range was expanded to include six other cars with racing heritages every bit as good as the XK120 – the MG TF, Austin Healey 100, Aston Martin DB2, Jaguar 2.4 saloon, Maserati 250F and Ferrari 375.

The MG TF could trace its racing pedigree back through the whole MG 'T' series to 1936 and beyond. The 'T' series had been raced all over the world,

including (in modified forms) at Le Mans, by some of the world's foremost racing drivers, such as Briggs Cunningham and Phil Hill, the first American to win the World Championship.

Although a stable-mate of the TF when British motor manufacturers the Nuffield Corporation and the Austin Motor Company merged to form BMC, the Austin Healey 100 was one of the cars that spelt the end for the MG. The MG's prewar styling looked positively antique compared to the Healey and the XK120. The Healey had the performance to go with its looks, too. It raced successfully worldwide, competing at Sebring in Florida and in the Bahamas with Stirling Moss at the wheel. It also featured at Le Mans.

The Aston Martin DB2 was a thoroughbred sports racing car which regularly tussled with the great XK120 on circuits around the world and helped to establish Aston Martin's glamorous image long before that upstart Bond came on the scene.

In 1955 Jaguar added the 2.4 saloon to its range and almost immediately began to dominate saloon car racing with what would become known as the Mark I. Along with its successor, the Mark II, it would become infamous as the favoured getaway car of assorted villains, blaggers and armed robbers who found they could easily outrun the local constabulary. The cops eventually turned the tables, however, when they too adopted the Jag.

Two Grand Prix cars completed the Scalex line-up, the Maserati 250F as driven by racing legend Juan Manuel Fangio to his fifth World Championship crown, and what has been listed as the Scalex Ferrari 4.5L, most probably a version of the 4-litre Ferrari 375 as driven by such legendary drivers as Ascari, Villoresi and Gonzalez. These were the cars of every schoolboy's dreams, and every

Left The special edition Blow
Out kit reaches the end
of the production line

Right The first Scalextric sets had no hand controls, just a button on the terminal box that switched the power to your car on or off

Left String power supplied the propulsion for the Startex cars. In the case of the Sunbeam Alpine, that meant tugging on the steering wheel

time they fired one up by dragging it back along the floor and let it go shooting off (well, trundling along for a few feet, anyway) they imagined themselves at the wheel, skidding round a mountain pass in the Alps or thundering past a cheering crowd in the grandstand at Monza, Reims or Monaco.

And the Scalex cars sold well, too. At one point they were producing up to 7,000 per week. Later models had front wheels which could be 'steered' by setting them at an angle so that, rather than following a straight line, the car would run in an arc – you'd have to be really lucky to get it to complete a whole circle.

These first cars, though, established a kind of 1:32 (1:28 in the case of the Ferrari and Maserati) scale sporting pedigree which would be reflected in all of the most successful of Scalextric's later models. You wouldn't expect to see a Scalextric Rolls-Royce or double-decker bus. The cars are, and have always been, about racing and high-speed action.

Running on String Power

Hot on the heels of Scalex came a new development called Startex. Instead of the fifth wheel winding the motor, these cars relied on a pull-cord. The idea was simple enough – pull the string, release it, and off goes the car with the string being wound in again as it goes. This system must surely have shattered a few illusions. The fifth wheel was invisible, so the cars looked just like they were racing along, but a car trailing a string really isn't going to look the part, is it? All the more so when the end of the pull-cord is (in the case of the Austin Healey and Jaguar 2.4) the car's exhaust pipe. A glamorous racing car loses a lot of its dignity when it's trailing its exhaust pipe on a piece of string

and, worse still, sucking the whole lot up its rear end as though it's in some bizarre spaghetti-eating contest.

A new Startex model, the Sunbeam Alpine, based on a car which had notable successes in the Alpine Rally, had the pull-cord attached to its oversized steering wheel. Trailing your exhaust pipe along behind you isn't an unknown occurrence; the exhaust can fall off without causing you too much agitation. Trailing your steering wheel behind you, however, is another matter. That would be cause for some real concern. Active imaginations, on the other hand, fly too high for minor earthly details to cause any distraction, so it's unlikely that any child playing with the Startex cars cared too much about the aesthetics of the new winding mechanism.

It's also unlikely, therefore, that the cord had much to do with the plug being pulled on the Scalex/Startex cars. Sales had started to tail off by the time Mr Francis, who was certainly shrewd enough to understand that new product lines are

Above A punishment cell for errant drivers? No, just a cunningly disguised battery housing

The drivers' bizarrely moulded hands didn't leave them with much chance of keeping the tin-plate Maserati **(left)** and Ferrari **(right)** under control

the key to success in the toy business, spotted something which inspired his next project. In 1956, he saw a demonstration of electric toy cars on their own road system, and realised how easily his own cars could be adapted and fitted with electric motors.

In January 1957, Scalextric (*Scalex* cars with elec*tric* power) was launched, and although recognisably the same sort of system it was a far cry from the sophistication of today's version.

The first cars were tin-plate Maserati 250F models adapted from the Scalex range, and they ran on a rubber track which simply pushed together and was even more simply pulled apart when the family dog, your drunken uncle or your granny (drunk or sober) blundered into it. Track clips underneath

Above The electrical pick-up on the original Scalextric cars was a solid wheel which slotted into the track rather than the later 'brushes'

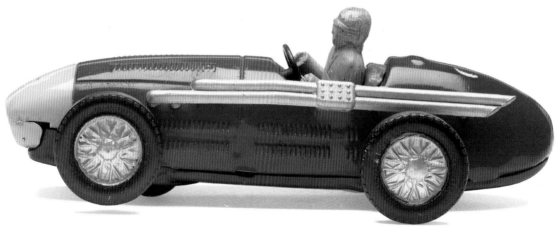

Above As if having deformed hands wasn't enough, the exhaust on the Maserati was close enough to melt the driver's whole arm off

would help hold your circuit together, but not much.

The cars also had a little rubber driver whose hands were so strangely moulded that they looked incapable of doing up his flies let alone wrestling with the steering wheel of his racing car. This wasn't important though. The imagination came into its own again and the Scalextric set turned the living-room floor into a racing arena fit for heroes.

Hand throttles that allowed you to control your

car's speed were still three years away. All you had was an on/off button which either gave you juice to your motor, or no juice. Since your set would undoubtedly be powered by batteries, no juice to your motor would be the only option after about an hour's racing. The batteries were housed in a little cardboard hut which looked for all the world like a prison block for naughty drivers (although quite what villainy they could get up to with hands like that is a bit of a puzzle) and battery power could easily fail when you were leading by a mile, halfway through the last lap of the deciding round in the Grand Prix World Championship. Oh, the frustration, the tantrums, the howling and wailing. And the kids were just as bad.

Buying a transformer/rectifier was the only answer, and battery power would become a thing of the past by the early Sixties.

Despite its shortcomings, this new slot-car racing toy was the best thing around, and it was an instant hit. Orders flooded in to Minimodels and

production was under way by May 1957. The Scalex Ferrari and Austin Healey were adapted to join the range and a year after the first Scalextric sets were produced it became clear to Mr Francis that he had become a victim of his own success. The volume of business was now such that he either had to spend a great deal of money expanding Minimodels to cope with increased production levels, or sell out to a bigger concern. In November 1958 Mr Francis sold Minimodels to the Tri-ang Group.

Tri-ang immediately put a wide range of important revisions in hand, and by the time the first new models of the new regime were ready to race, Scalextric as we know it today would be sitting in pole position.

Left You might have preferred to have your Ferrari in racing red but the driver would have preferred to have a seatbelt and he didn't get what he wanted either

Fantastic Plastic

Tri-ang took Scalextric racing into the Sixties with the pedal to the metal, or rather pedal to the plastic, because the first cars in the new Tri-ang range were moulded plastic, instantly recognisable as the predecessors of today's cars. The manufacturing process may have been right up to date, the 1960s were without doubt the plastic age, but the cars were a couple of years behind the times. Given that you can't design, tool up and manufacture a model car before the manufacturer of the real item has launched the real thing and let you see what it's going to look like, naturally Scalextric models have always lagged a little behind their full-size counterparts.

The new models were only a couple of years

Right A veteran Vanwall being put through its paces at the 1995 Goodwood Festival of Speed

behind the times and that could hardly have mattered for living-room racers who, though these were the swinging Sixties, were still accustomed to seeing cars of the Forties and Fifties on the street. The revolutionary car designs of the new modern era were yet to come.

Although 1960 saw the proliferation of mid-engined Formula 1 cars, Scalextric fans would certainly have been more familiar with the two Grand Prix stalwarts offered in the new (and concise at only four pages) Scalextric catalogue – the Vanwall VW10 and the Lotus 16.

The Vanwall had finished its competitive career in 1958, when Vanwall took the Formula 1 Constructors' Cup with Stirling Moss winning the last Grand Prix of the season at Casablanca in Morocco. The Vanwall team officially withdrew from racing in 1958, although a Vanwall car was seen in competition over the next couple of years in the hands of Tony Brooks, who had formerly driven for Vanwall.

The only Vanwall still known to be in working order is, in fact, the car that Moss drove in 1958. It was sold at an auction of historic racing cars at the

Right The Vanwall, as driven by Stirling Moss, was one of Scalextric's first Formula 1 cars

Colin Chapman's Lotus team entered the Formula 1 fray in 1958 with the Lotus 16, which looked remarkably similar to the Vanwall, unashamedly drawing inspiration from its fellow British worldbeater. The Lotus 16 never really achieved the same level of performance as the Vanwall, and even future world champion Graham Hill couldn't coax a Grand Prix win out of it.

The Scalextric Lotus 16 and Vanwall were far more evenly matched on the track. Lighter and faster than the previous tin-plate models, they had a new Tri-ang Rovex motor which was advertised in the first catalogue as being 'TV suppressed'. That meant that the kids could be battling it out behind the sofa without the electric motors harming the TV reception as Mum sat down to watch trendy Ken Barlow scandalise his family by taking part in a 'ban the bomb' march in the UK's new TV soap, *Coronation Street*. In America, where Scalextric was already making inroads, the new plastic cars had even greater competition for attention as John F Kennedy took on his rival for the US presidency in the first-ever televised head-to-head debate of its kind. My guess is Scalextric won.

Nürburgring in 1998 for almost £900,000. An original Scalextric version of the Vanwall is much sought after but isn't likely to stretch the purse strings quite so far. You might pay £40 for a pristine example – still a major price hike for a model that was retailing in 1961 for under £1.10s (£1.50).

Left The Lotus 16 was the Vanwall's Scalextric stablemate

Along with the new bodywork and motor, the 1960 cars also had a new kind of locator to fit into the track slot. Rather than the old 'wheel', this was a pin device with loops of wire braid at either side. It helped to keep the new cars on the track, as did the new hand controllers. The hand throttles allowed you to take the car from a standing start up to full speed as well as to slow down for the corners, just like today's versions, although unlike the more modern 'trigger' throttle, these original controls fitted into the palm of the hand, and the throttle was controlled by pushing your thumb down on a spring-loaded plunger.

In fact, the basics of today's system were now all in place and the earliest Scalextric cars from 1957 will actually run on today's track, just as today's cars will run on the early track, so slight have been the fundamental changes in the system over almost half a century.

Above Early hand controls with plunger-style throttles

Right Catalogue No 2 – now a hefty 24 pages

Two more cars became available later in the year, the Lister Jaguar and Aston Martin DBR.

Brian Lister's Jaguars helped to keep the great British marque in motor sport after Jaguar officially retired from competition in 1956, and the Scalextric Lister is a version of his 1959 car, which saw service at Sebring, the Nürburgring and Le Mans as well as countless other sports car and endurance races.

Just as the Vanwall was aptly pitted against the Lotus, the Lister Jaguar was teamed with its real-life sparring partner, the Aston Martin DBR. DBRs had been racing in various forms since 1956, with

Above The Scalextric D-type Jaguar lacked the 'fin' of the real thing but wasn't actually inaccurate because of it

Left The Lister Jaguar cars kept the famous British marque's racing flag flying after the company retired from motorsport

world-famous drivers like Roy Salvadori bringing Aston Martin the World Sports Car Championship as well as a win at Le Mans in 1959. Unusually for a sports racer of the time, the exhaust pipe on the DBR cars ran underneath the car and exited at the back rather than running outside the car and exiting at the side. This meant that the floor of the car could become extremely hot during races and nobody could ever accuse DBR drivers of having cold feet!

Running a little on the hot side was also a problem for Scalextric cars and a word of caution was given at the front of their first full-length (24-page) catalogue in 1961, advising that 'no motor will go flat-out for ever – so rest cars now and then if there is any sign of overheating. (A spare is a good thing to have, the fun can continue unabated . . .).'

Racing the cars until they were hotter and sweatier than Roy Salvadori's feet just wouldn't have been possible in the bad old days of battery power, although battery power was still an option in 1961.

In the year that Jaguar launched its sensational E-type, Scalextric introduced its version of the

phenomenal D-type. The D-type had famously won at Le Mans three years running in 1955, 56 and 57. It rocketed from a standing start to 60 mph in less than 4 seconds and could reach a top speed of around 190 mph. The 1957 Le Mans win came a year after Jaguar withdrew from motor sport, although the company still lent its support to the teams which entered the five D-types. All five cars finished, taking an incredible first, second, third, fourth and sixth places.

In America the blue and white racing colours of the Briggs Cunningham team adorned the D-type when it roared to victory on its first US outing in the Sebring 12-hour race in 1955. From then on the mere sight of the sleek Jaguars with the distinctive tail fin would cause dismay in the paddocks of raceways all over the country. Every driver knew that with a D-type on the starting grid they were in for a tough race.

That distinctive tail fin has caused some consternation among Scalextric fans, because on Scalextric's version of the car, the fin is missing. In fact, when the D-type was first tested at Le Mans

Above The Porsche 550 –
140 mph from less
than 1500 cc

before the 1954 event, it had no fin. The three cars which ran unsuccessfully in the 1954 race had the fins added to give them stability at speed when it was realised just how fast the D-type would go. In testing the non-finned version at Le Mans, Tony Rolt beat Alberto Ascari's 1953 lap record by 3 seconds. The Scalextric D-type is actually a pretty accurate rendition of Rolt's car.

Table Topping in America

Two Grand Prix racers were also added to the Scalextric stable in 1961, both highly respected British cars. Britain was producing cars at the cutting edge of motor-sport technology and, with changing attitudes and a new spirit of optimism, Britain was the place to be. The Beatles staged their first performance at the now legendary Cavern Club in Liverpool, fashions which would later become instantly recognisable as 'Sixties' were starting to hit the streets, and the new contraceptive pill was causing almost as much controversy as it was damage to the bedsprings.

The British teams whose cars appeared in Scalextric form were Cooper and BRM. Both teams had extensive racing histories, and in 1959

Cooper had won both the Constructors' Cup and produced a British World Champion in Jack Brabham with the Cooper T51, the model now available from Scalextric.

BRM had seen more than its fair share of ups and downs over the previous twenty years, but with Graham Hill putting up a spirited performance in the British Grand Prix in 1960 at Silverstone, they were showing that they were a force to be reckoned with. The Scalextric offering was the BRM 25, the car that had given BRM its first Grand Prix win at Zandvoort in 1959.

Perhaps the most interesting Scalextric newcomer, though, wasn't British but German – the Porsche Spyder. The model was based on Porsche's 550 series which had been introduced eight years earlier and had won on its first outing at the Nürburgring in May 1953. It then went on to finish fifteenth at Le Mans and first in its class (in fact it was the only finisher in its class). Throughout the 1950s, 550s continued to race in various forms, both open (Spyder) and coupé, taking first in class at Reims, in the Carrera Panamericana and in Buenos Aires, to name but a few. In 1955 they finished fourth, fifth and sixth at Le Mans, naturally winning first in class again. It was in the gruelling Targa Florio race that the 550A variant really proved its mettle, though, winning outright and finishing 15 minutes ahead of its nearest rival.

All this makes the car pretty special, even more so when you consider that it had an engine of less than 1500 cc but could reach speeds of around 140 mph. And the Spyder drivers never went hungry due to all of the flies in their teeth.

On the Scalextric track the Spyder made for an aggressive-looking coupling racing against the D-type. On a real racing circuit it would have struggled a bit against the more powerful Jag, but plastic bodies and electric motors are great levellers!

The new cars were eagerly awaited in America, where Scalextric was being pushed hard by specialist retailers such as Polk's Hobbies of Fifth Avenue, New York. 'If you're looking for a hobby that won't go stale . . . table top racing, the fastest growing hobby sport, is for you!' is how they promoted Scalextric in advertisements in the motoring press. Their boxed sets, which included two cars, track hand controllers, etc, were being offered at $49.95 for the most expensive version

had puffed up its chest enough to reach 140 in real life. This 130 mph scale speed sounds amazing but, given that the cars were to a scale of 1:32, that means that they were hurtling round the track at an actual speed of just over 4 mph. Nothing too much for the traffic cops to worry about there, then. Still, figures like that are fuel to fire the imagination, throwing down a challenge and maintaining the fun element of Scalextric. Keeping your car on the track and winning races at a scale speed of 130 mph gets the adrenalin flowing, whereas pottering round to win a 4 mph race is somewhat less exciting . . . and

Left Scalextric's Porsche Spyder was sometimes fitted with a lead weight in the rear to improve its handling

(plus $1 postage if you bought mail order). The same kind of set would have been sold in the UK for around £12.

Polk's also highlighted the fact that 'skill and daring win races' at scale speeds of 130 mph – something of an insult to the little Porsche which

losing a 4 mph race. Well, you'd never dare to show your face in Monaco again.

In May 1961 Scalextric manufacturing was moved to a new, purpose-built factory in Havant, Hampshire, not far from the previous premises. Continual improvements were sought in the

Above Was the Bentley driver glancing right to judge the apex of the corner and keep the racing line . . . or was he just looking snooty?

production process, leading to more accurate detailing in the mouldings and the most elaborate plastic cars yet produced – the new models for 1962 were vintage racing cars. The catalogue announced them as being modelled on cars displayed at the Montagu Motor Museum at Beaulieu in Hampshire.

The big Bentleys had dominated Le Mans in the 1920s and 30s, winning outright in 1924, 1927 and 1928, taking first, second and third places in 1929 and first and second in 1930. This was with cars ranging from 3-litre engine capacity to 6.5 litres, with potential top speeds ranging accordingly from just under 100 mph to just over 140 mph. The amazing Bentleys were the stuff of *Boy's Own* stories, monstrously large, cumbersome beasts with an aristocratic air of power and superiority that they reinforced with crushing victories on the road. The indelicate nature of the cars was what led Ettore Bugatti famously to comment that, 'My friend Monsieur Bentley builds the fastest lorries of anyone I know.'

Ironically, the Scalextric model of a '1928 4.5 litre super-charged Bentley, Le Mans replica body.

Engine: 4 cylinder' was one of the less successful models, the supercharger rendering the engine rather less reliable than its 'unblown' counterparts. Nevertheless, it was still a formidable machine.

Taking over where Bentley left off was the new Alfa Romeo 8C with its highly advanced, 4-cylinder 2.3-litre engine. The Scalextric model was a touring sports variant, but the same engine enlarged to 2.6 litres powered the 'Monza' sports racers and P3 Grand Prix machines. At the time, the race everyone wanted to win was Le Mans and the Alfas duly did so in 1931, 1932 (first, second and third), 1933 (same again) and 1934. The Alfa's

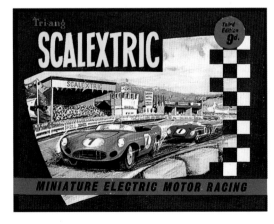

Right All-action front cover of the 1962 catalogue

1-2-3 victory in 1932 was achieved with the lead car averaging 76.5 mph for the race, around 10 per cent faster than the 4.5-litre Bentley of 1928.

Scalextric electric motors, as always, put the advantage in the hand of the racer with the most skilful thumb when these vintage warriors rubbed wheels on the slotted track.

The Typhoon sidecar outfit **(left)** differed from the later Hurricane version **(above)** by, among other things, having no front wheel

Prayer Mats & Plastic Legs

Another new departure for Scalextric in 1962 was motorcycle racing. The Typhoon motorcycle and sidecar combinations ran on the normal track, when you could keep them on the track. They were so light and had so little grip that if you didn't control the speed with the skill of a real motorcyclist you would either tip the thing over or have it spinning round through 180° to start heading in the opposite direction.

If the Typhoon looked bizarre, then it was no more so than the real rigs raced in motorcycle and sidecar events. They hugged the ground closer than worm's knees and stood on the tarmac at only around 30 in tall. The sidecars were known as 'kneelers' or 'prayer mats' and the sidecar passenger's job was to stop the thing from tipping over or spinning round through 180° to start heading in the opposite direction. Hmmm . . . sounds familiar.

Rather than just using his thumb, however, the real sidecar passenger had to use every bit of his body, every ounce of his weight. He would lean out overboard like a racing yachtsman to keep the rig on the ground as it sped round a corner one way then clamber like an acrobat over behind the rider to lean out over the other side for the next turn. All that with

Left Was the Alfa Romeo driver looking left to judge the apex of the corner and keep the racing line . . . or was he spitting at the snooty Bentley driver?

Above The Auto Union, Hitler's favourite Scalextric car

proving ground for Formula 1 drivers of the future, but the Scalextric Go-Karts suffered from the same problems as the motorcycle and sidecar combinations. They were too light and unstable to race flat-out the way that people were coming to expect they could with the more conventional models.

The Go-Karts did, however, offer something that no other Scalextric model had – drivers with legs. In a traditional Le Mans start, where drivers have to sprint across the track to their waiting cars, the Go-Kart drivers would have had a huge advantage, as most of the other Scalextric drivers' bodies ended at their armpits. The original 1960 plastic car drivers, in fact, didn't even have arms and these are now referred to, in a strangely sinister way, as 'The Big Head'.

Go-Karts aside, 1963 was a time of glamour, innovation and excitement. Scotsman Jim Clark became Formula I World Champion in a Lotus 25, Craig Breedlove cracked the 400 mph land-speed barrier and the Beatles had three consecutive US No.1 hit singles when 'Can't Buy Me Love' replaced 'She Loves You' which had replaced 'I Wanna Hold Your Hand'. No doubt all three were surreptitiously recorded by a Dutch boffin as Philips put the final touches to their new-fangled cassette-tape machine.

Scalextric's contribution to the glamour came in the form of the Ferrari 250GT and Aston Martin DB4 GT. The Ferrari, predecessor to the mighty GTO, was a beautiful sight as it soared around the world's racetracks with a 3-litre V12 engine spiriting it up to a top speed of around 145 mph.

The Aston Martin was also the predecessor to a famous car, James Bond's notorious DB5. The DB4 GT may have lacked some of the optional

his nose and elbows skimming the tarmac. The rider pointed the thing in the right direction, changed the gears and took all the credit.

The new breed of mid-engined Formula 1 cars had not gone unnoticed by Scalextric and in 1962 they introduced the Ferrari 156 'sharknose' and Lotus 21. These two cars had fought some hard battles on the Formula 1 circuits the previous year and were involved in one of motor sport's greatest tragedies when Jim Clark's Lotus and the Ferrari of Wolfgang von Trips came together at Monza and the Ferrari was catapulted into the crowd, killing von Trips and 15 spectators and injuring many more.

Anxious to cover as many forms of motor sport as possible, Scalextric introduced Go-Karts for the first time in 1963. Real karting was by now a serious racing sport and would become a

extras fitted to Bond's later car, but it was certainly no slouch on the track. The performance from its 6-cylinder, 3.7-litre engine was similar to the Ferrari's, although it was more brutish as a racer.

Innovation? Both the Ferrari and the Aston Martin had working headlights, which wasn't an entirely new idea for Scalextric, lights having first

been introduced a couple of years earlier on the Lister Jaguar, but it did add to the overall glamour of the two new GT cars. The real innovation came with the introduction of the Cooper and Lotus Formula Junior cars which, although they looked fairly rudimentary, had sprung suspension and would 'steer' themselves round corners. The rudimentary

looks probably said more about the actual models, though, as did their price of around 16/- (£0.80), just over half the cost of the regular cars.

And excitement? What could be better than two new additions to the vintage racing car collection – Auto Union and Bugatti?

The Auto Union C-type was a revolutionary racing car of its time. Designed by Ferdinand Porsche for a company which was an amalgamation of four motor manufacturers (including Audi) represented by Auto Union's four-ringed emblem, the company received state funding from Adolf Hitler to turn Professor Porsche's designs for a mid-engined racer into a worldbeater. Government-backed racing teams, of course, were not an unknown phenomenon, but the deep economic crisis in Germany which had been Hitler's springboard to power was causing a national depression which the Führer was determined to lift. Parading Germany's mastery of technology on the racetracks of the world was one way to help restore national pride, Hitler subsidised two teams which

Left The cover for catalogue 4 showed how the motorcycle and sidecar combinations looked through the bottom of a beer glass

Below 1963's Go-Kart drivers had good legs and didn't mind showing them off

Above and below The Bugatti Type 59 was originally produced in limited numbers. When Scalextric racer Chris Gregory spotted a test moulding while visiting the factory to race against a team from Trinidad and Tobago, he put the word around and collector Steve DeHavilland persuaded Scalextric to produce a few car bodyshells for enthusiasts to create new versions of the original models. These became known as 'The DeHavilland Bugattis'

would compete in the all-silver national racing livery, Auto Union and Mercedes.

The Auto Union's V16 4.4-litre supercharged engine was mounted behind the driver but in front of the rear wheels, predating the layout of the first modern Grand Prix cars by more than 25 years. The A-type first raced in 1934, winning the German, Swiss and Hungarian Grands Prix. The next year the team fielded a revised B-type that won on their first Grand Prix outing at Tunis and went on to gain an impressive array of wins and places including first and second place at Pescara, where one of the Auto Unions was timed at over 180 mph.

The C-type on which the Scalextric model is based appeared in 1936 and was the most successful of the three variants, dominating the Grand Prix circuits with first, second and third places at Coppa Acerbo and the Swiss Grand Prix. With barely any modification, the cars ran again in 1937 and again were a force to be reckoned with, their strongest opposition coming from Hitler's other favourites, the Mercedes W125s. Among their 1937 Grand Prix successes, the Auto Unions won at Donington in the UK and triumphed in the US Vanderbilt Cup race.

The Bugatti name reeks of racing history, having been at the forefront of motor sport throughout the 1920s and 30s, perhaps the most exciting period in motor racing. The car which Scalextric offered in 1963 was the Bugatti Type 59, the last of Bugatti's Grand Prix racers. Always keen

to apply the latest technological innovations to his creations, Ettore Bugatti took inspiration from America's sensational Miller cars to create an 8-cylinder, 3.3-litre, supercharged engine that would power the Type 59 to first, second and fourth places in the 1934 Belgian Grand Prix as well as a win at Algiers.

The great opposition, of course, came from the silver German cars, but the Type 59 proved its mettle, remaining competitive for several years and breaking the record for cars of its class at Brooklands when it lapped the famous banked circuit at almost 140 mph.

The beautifully detailed Bugatti, in its original form, has become one of the cars that Scalextric collectors covet most. Although it was intended, along with the Auto Union, to expand the vintage car collection, Scalextric made only a few hundred examples. Perhaps, with the Sixties in full swing,

living-room racers only wanted to see modern cars and demand just wasn't there. The fact that the vintage collection wasn't expanded to include more new models tends to bear this out.

Scalextric's World Champion

Jim Clark had taken seven victories from the ten championship Grand Prix events to become World Champion in 1963 and bring the Constructors' Cup to Lotus. He would continue to race for Lotus in 1964, but also signed to another team – Scalextric. Having the World Champion on board to promote what was being advertised as 'the most complete model motor racing system in the world' was surely the best endorsement that Scalextric could have, and business went from strength to strength. Scalextric models were in production in Tri-ang factories in France, Australia and New Zealand and a manufacturing and distribution agreement was reached with a Spanish company. In America, Scalextric joined forces with a company called Lionel, which produced model trains, to expand upon the sales which had already been achieved there.

And international influence was not limited to sales. The previous three years' catalogues had supplied advice and encouragement in the field of organising races, printing a list of 'General Racing Notes' on the back page, and fans could write to the Scalextric Association Secretary at the Tri-ang/Minimodels factory in Hampshire for details about how to set up their own Scalextric Club. Within a very short time, local Scalextric clubs would spring up all over the country, and the network would quickly go global, infecting communities all over the world with the model motor racing craze that was so compulsive it was almost sinister.

In fact, if some devious device for mind control and manipulation could have been developed, then Scalextric would surely have been the ideal addictive delivery system. Secret Service Agent 007's old adversaries at SPECTRE would have cooked up the plot, of course, just as they had done in the first two Bond movies. However, the Bond adventure that had some US cinemas opening 24 hours a day to cope with the unprecedented demand for tickets featured a new Bond villain, Goldfinger. Included in the special equipment issued

Right 1964's front cover was a dramatic piece of artwork

to 007 for the Goldfinger assignment was the fabulous Aston Martin DB5, more of which later.

Consolidating the theme of world domination, Scalextric racers from bedrooms, garages, Scout huts and community centres far and wide gathered in London in 1964 for the first Scalextric World Championship. So successful was the event that it would subsequently be staged every two years right into the 1970s.

The international success of Scalextric was set against a rolling background of cultural and scientific development in a world that was changing faster even than the batteries on the original racing sets. America's Ranger 7 probe was beaming pictures to earth from the Moon, Donald Campbell set a new World Land Speed record of 403.1 mph, Diana Ross made her first TV appearance with the Supremes on the *Ed Sullivan Show*, and if Scalextric executives needed help in keeping up with the sales figures of their new models, Japanese electronics company Sharp introduced the desk-top calculator.

The new Scalextric models unveiled in 1964 included two Formula 1 cars. The BRM 51 was the car in which Graham Hill became 1962 World Champion and brought BRM the Constructors' Cup. The Porsche 804 was the car in which Dan Gurney won his (and Porsche's) first Grand Prix at Rouen in France in 1962. In the pits there was jubilation among an unlikely bunch of hairy wild men. The Porsche mechanics had sworn not to shave until their car finally won a Grand Prix. They'd be tripping over their beards before Porsche won another one.

A new version of the Aston Martin DB4 GT also

appeared (not the one with the machine guns and ejector seat – yet), with a roof light to add to its other illuminations and flags attached to the front and rear bumpers. The car was in black (although a red version was also produced) and had the word 'MARSHAL' on the side. No, not a Federal Marshal, but a track marshal, the kind who are sent out onto racetracks to take charge and, if necessary, slow the race to a halt when an accident makes it too dangerous to continue. It's difficult to tell what could make that necessary in a Scalextric race. Teatime? Bedtime? Pet hamster on the track? Anyone who tried to use the Scalextric car to interrupt a race wouldn't be very popular and, despite the fact that it

Above The Big Healey – 'last of the hairy-chested British sports cars'

was a handsome model, it was doubtless shunted, rammed and forced off the track at every opportunity. The ensuing damage would have been considerable, and that may go some way towards explaining why collectors nowadays get so very excited when they come across an example which is still intact and complete with both of its flags.

The final two additions to the 1964 Scalextric line-up were the Mercedes 190SL and Austin Healey 3000 sports racing cars.

The German car had first appeared in 1955 as

Above The Timekeeper's Hut from 1962 featured an electric hooter to let you know when the race was over

Right By 1964, Scalextric enjoyed the endorsement of World Champion Jim Clark and his image appeared on the cover of the 1965 catalogue

a smaller sister to the famous 300SL, the revolutionary gull-wing car which had won first time out at Le Mans in the first year that Mercedes Benz returned to sports car racing after World War II. The 190SL was an altogether less sophisticated machine, with conventional doors rather than the gull-wing variety used on the 300SL. As the number designation would suggest, it had a 1900 cc engine as opposed to the 300SL's 3-litre but it could still top 100 mph and gave a good account of itself in road and track races for its class. The 190SL remained in production up to 1963. The Scalextric version would eventually have the distinction of carrying a passenger alongside the driver when it took on a very special role alongside 007's Aston Martin with a spectacular optional extra all of its own . . .

BMC's Austin Healey 3000 was derived from the earlier 100S and 100-Six models and has often been described as the 'last of the hairy-chested British sports cars', implying that its brutish power and uncompromising handling characteristics required a strong-armed racing driver with muscles

SCALEXTRIC
MODEL ELECTRIC MOTOR RACING
REGD.
SIXTH EDITION

bursting out of the sleeves of his racing overalls (and presumably, chest hair out of the open neck) to keep the car in check. That would be no way to describe a lady like Pat Moss who, along with Ann Wisdom, won the Rome–Liège–Rome rally outright in a 'Big Healey' in 1960 and took the car to second place in the RAC rally the following year.

There was no doubt, however, that for a sports car it could be a heavy and cumbersome beast, though that didn't stop it from dominating rallies where the conditions suited it, especially at the hands of protagonists such as Timo Makinen or Don and Erle Morley, who won the prestigious Coupe des Alpes in 1961, 62 and 64.

By 1966 the car was losing out to smaller, more nimble rally cars, but it had earned the affection of sports car enthusiasts and, although original 1960s Big Healeys have always sold well in the classic car market, the popularity of its styling has recently led to it being remanufactured as

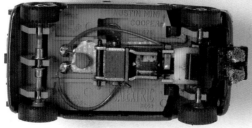

Right The 1965 Scalextric Mini Cooper had front wheel drive **(bottom)** but didn't handle as well as later rear-wheel-drive versions **(top)**

the HMC, a bespoke, hand-built motor with modern engineering refinements but the same handsome exterior.

Ironically, one of the cars that spelt the end for the Big Healey's sporting career was its BMC stablemate and the only new Scalextric car for 1965, the Mini Cooper. Ever since it was launched in 1959, designer Sir Alec Issigonis's ingenious little car had had sporting pretensions, and it would go on to have one of the longest and most distinguished racing careers of any car in the world. Indeed, at the 1960 British Grand Prix at Silverstone, a demonstration race was staged for fun, all of the combatants driving Minis and all of the top Formula 1 stars involved, including Jim Clark, Phil Hill, John Surtees, Jo Bonnier, Innes Ireland, Bruce McLaren and Graham Hill.

The Mini Cooper came about when race team maestro John Cooper, a friend of Issigonis, modified the standard model specifically for competition. It had a larger engine than the original (997 cc as opposed to 850 cc), producing enough

power to make the humble Mini highly competitive, even against some of the world's most exotic sports cars. Engine sizes and general specifications would change over the years as the Mini's haul of international trophies continued to grow. One of its early successes came in 1962 when Pat Moss and Ann Wisdom won the Coupe des Dames at the Monte Carlo Rally. The Mini would ultimately take its first outright win in the Monte in 1964 at the hands of Paddy Hopkirk, battling against fantastically powerful opposition from his nearest rival in a mighty Ford Galaxie. The Mini won the Monte again in 1965 with Timo Makinen at the

Right 1966's catalogue front cover put the reader behind the wheel of Jim Clark's Lotus

Below The 1968 Mini Coopers had a rather fragile spotlight on the roof

Above and right The Ford GT 40, four times Le Mans winner

Below Scalextric was available in kit form in 1966 with this AC Cobra and a Porsche 904 model

wheel, and would have made it three in a row in 1966 but for some incredibly complicated rule-juggling by the French authorities, who eventually awarded the prize to a Citroën. The Minis got their own back in 1967 when they returned in force and Rauno Aaltonen drove his Mini to victory.

As well as scrabbling round rally routes, Minis were perfectly at home in the muddy fields of rallycross circuits or on tarmac racetracks, where they proved their speed and agility countless times, winning the British as well as the European Touring Car Championships.

By the time the Scalextric Mini Cooper was scurrying round the slotted track, there were already 1 million of the full-size version on the road. The original Scalextric model was, like the full-sized car, front-wheel drive, but this arrangement didn't produce the best performance and the models were subsequently given a more conventional (for Scalextric) rear-wheel-drive layout.

Jim Clark's endorsement of Scalextric continued through 1965 as he regained his World Championship title, becoming Formula 2 champion at the same time and the first non-American to win the Indy 500 into the bargain. But it wasn't all champagne and glory for the Scotsman, as he explained in his introduction to the 1966 Scalextric catalogue: 'My one regret is that in my early youth there was no Scalextric and I did not have the opportunity that you, the Champion of tomorrow, now has to build replicas of famous circuits in your own home.'

Feeling perhaps a little more buoyant than the apparently deeply depressed Jim Clark, John Lennon announced in 1966 that the Beatles were 'more popular than Jesus', The Monkees had a No.1 hit in the US with 'I'm A Believer', Graham Hill won the Indy 500 in a Lola and England won the soccer World Cup at Wembley.

If all of that and the fact that *Thunderbirds* started on ITV wasn't enough to gladden any youngster's heart, then Scalextric had a bumper crop of new cars to offer.

The 1965 Scalextric range had offered a total of 23 different models, and for 1966 there would be 8 more including Jim Clark's Lotus 25 and Bruce McLaren's Cooper for Formula 1 fans.

Perhaps more interesting, though, were the models manufactured in Hong Kong with the American market in mind. Scalextric's relationship with Lionel had been bearing fruit and Americans were increasing their share of the slot-car market, although they naturally wanted to see cars more familiar to American racing fans. American motor racing certainly featured European cars, with works teams or works-assisted teams entering sports cars to help promote their production cars, but US 'open-wheeled' racing cars were a breed apart.

Two versions of the famous American Offenhauser circuit racer were offered, with renditions of both a front-engined and slightly more modern mid-engined model. The net was spread wider than just Indy-style cars, though, as the Ford GT 40 and AC Cobra were also made available.

The GT 40 must have seemed very much like America's answer to the glamorous Le Mans Ferraris and Porsches fielded by the Europeans but the car was actually much more British than American, built in a factory in Slough, totally separately from Ford's other UK plants. No matter where it originated, there was no denying its sensational performances. Launched in 1964, the

car was powered by a 4.7-litre V8 engine, although it was fitted with a 7-litre engine in 1965 for Le Mans, where it could reach 200 mph on the Mulsanne Straight. This failed to produce a victory that year but in 1966 (with a 5-litre engine), 67, 68 and 69 the GT 40 did take first place at Le Mans.

For most Americans, however, Le Mans was a far-off racecourse in a far-off land. They watched the big Ford thunder round racetracks much nearer home with another Ford-engined sports racer in hot pursuit. The AC Cobra was again devised in the UK (AC was a British company), but it was American driver and team racer Caroll Shelby who made the car such a winner on the racetrack. The original Cobras were powered by the American 4.7 litre Ford engine, although with a 6.9 litre powerplant, Shelby's car finished fourth at Le Mans in 1965. He

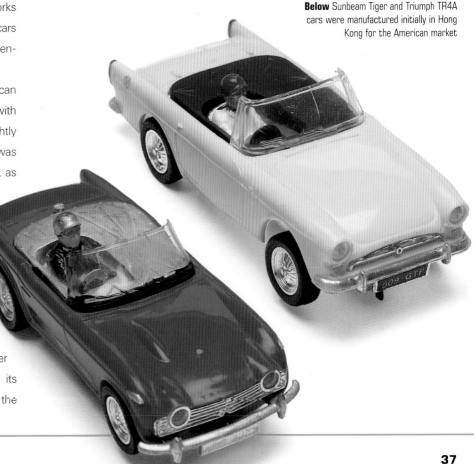

Below Sunbeam Tiger and Triumph TR4A cars were manufactured initially in Hong Kong for the American market

Right A buzzer would sound in 1965's penalty skid chicane if you hit one of the hazards. If something hit you, then you probably already knew about it

also won the American Manufacturers' Sports Car Championship for the second year running. Shelby fitted his own 'Daytona' coupé bodywork for the endurance races, and in the States the road cars (with a top speed of over 150 mph) bore a Shelby rather than an AC badge.

The last two Hong Kong Scalextric models were quintessential British sports cars but each was marketed heavily in the US and both were well known to American sports car enthusiasts.

The Triumph TR4A had Michelotti styling and a 2.1-litre engine which gave it a top speed of around 110 mph, enough for it to capitalise on the TR racing heritage and win the Alpine Rally in 1962.

It was a rugged and reliable club racer, too, happily at home hurtling round a racing circuit. It was launched into the American market, where Triumph had a long-established network of dealers, in 1964 and quickly won a substantial US following.

The TR had stiff competition in the American market that year from the new version of the Sunbeam Alpine, the Tiger. Like the AC Cobra, the Sunbeam Tiger was a British car with the immense American 4.2- (later 4.7-) litre Ford engine. It was immensely popular with club racers and was campaigned by Sunbeam in all of the most important rally events, even, in modified coupé form, running at Le Mans. Derived from the

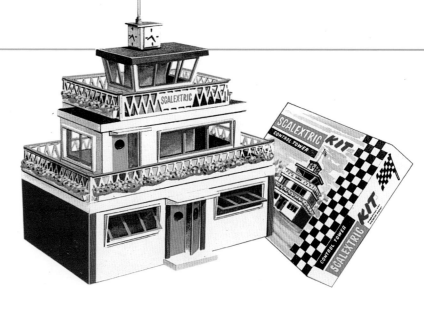

smaller-engined Sunbeam Alpine and looking almost identical, the Tiger stayed in production for barely three years, suffering badly in a company takeover which saw the Rootes Group (which owned Sunbeam) sell out to Chrysler. Well, Chrysler could hardly have a a showcase sports car powered by Ford, could they?

To cater for the highly developed skills of Scalextric drivers who might now have been racing for almost ten years, a selection of 1966 models was offered in 'Race Tuned' form. These cars had a specially modified electric motor which gave more speed but required a new type of 'Race Tuned' hand control, as the new cars would burn out the old throttles. The new control had been 'specially designed to operate high powered motors and incorporates a special braking device' and the whole 'Race Tuned' series was described as being suitable for 'the advanced Scalextric driver who needs more speed, instantaneous acceleration and perfect braking power'.

Hang on a minute. Isn't that all starting to sound a bit too serious? Scalextric cars aren't real racing cars, after all, are they? They're just toys.

Think again.

Scalextric had by now left behind the pit-lane status of 'mere toys' with wheels spinning and charged through the chicane of 'hobby interest', changing into top gear for the fast straight of 'competitive sport'. There was now even a Scalextric AC Cobra and Porsche 904 GTS offered in kit form for the enthusiast to build, paint and customise, with a choice of interchangeable rear-axle gears to suit different types of circuit.

All this meant that Mr Fun was in danger of taking a bit of a back seat, but there was a supreme piece of silliness just around the corner that would

see him climbing right back into the driver's seat again – the James Bond set was launched in 1967.

The most expensive two-car set then produced, 'The New Super Excitement James Bond Car Chase Set' featured track sections designed purely to send the cars smashing into each other at every conceivable opportunity. There were converging chicane sections leading into an entire chicane curve as well as a skid chicane, 90° crossover and . . . a boulder.

The villains' car, an adapted Mercedes 190SL, had two occupants, one of whom was waving a gun and fell out of the car so often that he might just as well have stood at the side of the track to shoot at 007 each time he came past. The main reason that

Above Kits such as this Control Tower cut the cost of redevelopment around your circuit

Below Grandstand Figures that you could paint yourself appeared in 1963. Painting yourself might not have been a bad idea if your hands were as colourless as this

SCALEXTRIC Regd.
MODEL MOTOR RACING
U.K. PRICE 1/-
EIGHTH EDITION

Mercedes get behind you and ram your rear
bumper, a bulletproof shield will pop up out of the
boot. Should you have an unwelcome passenger,
just drive past this revolving boulder in the road
which will turn a little each time you go by until it is
sitting at precisely the correct agle to trip this switch
on the side of the car which will activate the ejector
seat and shoot the little blighter out through your
sunroof. Oh, and do take good care of this
equipment when you are in the field, 007. It is
government property and we do want it back in
proper working order . . .'

Alas, when the ejector-seat switch was tripped
by the boulder, Bond's passenger shot out so fast
that he was more than likely to join his henchman
from the Mercedes in the darkest recesses of the
sofa and the Aston Martin's sunroof could end up
anywhere from the dog's bowl to your grandad's
cardigan pocket. Keeping the DB5 intact wasn't
really all that difficult, though, especially when it

he fell out so often (until he inevitably became lost
under the sofa for a couple of years) was that the
Mercedes had a spring-loaded wire arm under its
trunk which catapulted the car off the track
whenever Bond's car hit it in the rear bumper.

Ah, then there's Bond's Aston Martin DB5.
Q would have been delighted.

'Now pay attention, 007. Should the villains'

Left This catalogue illustration clearly shows that Goldfinger's henchman at some point had at least 1½ legs

promised the most fun you could ever have with a Scalextric set without shrinking yourself down to two inches high and driving the cars yourself.

Surprisingly, the 007 set didn't sell as well as was hoped (although a complete set is now a highly prized collectors' item), perhaps because the *Goldfinger* movie had been three years ago and the Aston Martin DB5 was only ever seen again briefly in *Thunderball* in 1965 until Pierce Brosnan's Bond revived it when he diced with Xenia Onatopp's Ferrari in *Goldeneye* 30 years later. The Bond movie for 1967, *You Only Live Twice*, featured a Toyota 2000 GT as its glamour car.

Towards the End of an Era

The paucity of new models in the 1967 catalogue was redressed for 1968 with a whole gridlock of new cars, some of which would have solicited appreciative and admiring glances in even the most uptown traffic jams and some of which would certainly have left other drivers scratching their heads a bit.

Below The 1968 catalogue heavily featured the Super 124 cars

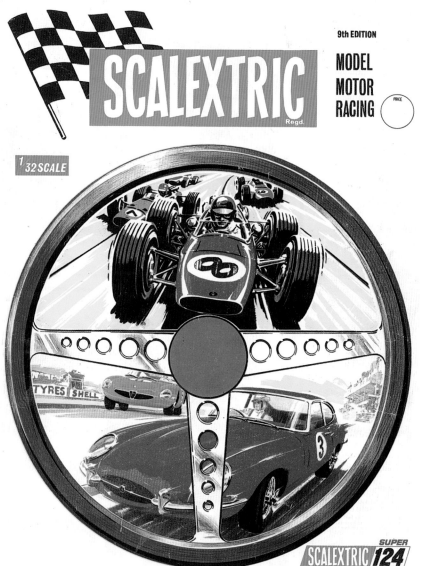

The 'Rally Mini Cooper', easily identifiable by the spotlight on the roof, was introduced with rear-wheel drive to help solve the handling problems of the original Scalextric Mini. Ironically, on the real Mini front-wheel drive was one of the things that made it so successful in motor sport. Having the weight of the engine over the drive wheels allowed for a more compact, well-balanced little car that could be thrown around corners in a manner that would leave other cars spinning on their roofs. Although the rear-wheel drive of the Scalextric Mini helped keep it on the track, over-enthusiasm in the thumb department would, as with all Scalextric cars, still result in a 'big off' and that cute little spotlight on the roof was often a sad casualty when the Mini was left . . . er . . . spinning on its roof.

The Mercedes 250SL was an altogether different kind of sports car. It was an updated, although visually very similar, version of the 230SL which Mercedes had launched at the Geneva motor show in 1963. Both the 230 and 250 were widely raced on the track as well as in rally events. At the hands of champion rally driver Eugen Böhringer, the works 230SL won the taxing Spa–Sofia–Liège rally in 1963, and Böhringer later proved how good both he and the SL were on the track when he showed everyone a clean pair of heels at the Nürburgring.

The Scalextric 250SL was manufactured by Scalextric's associate company in Spain where it had originally been marketed as the Mercedes 230SL (told you they looked the same!) along with the other of the first two Spanish-originated models, the SEAT 600. In the UK, the SEAT appeared in the 1968 catalogue as the Fiat 600. Like the Mini, the real-life Fiat 600 had been around since the late 1950s. Also like the Mini, it was a small car with a small engine that made a disproportionately large impact on the motor-sport scene. With its 633 cc engine giving it a top speed of just over 60 mph in standard form, though, the little plastic Spanish driver must have been intensely jealous of his cousin in the Mercedes. On the slotted track, however, they were as evenly matched as any Scalextric cars, which meant that the Fiat would be able to hit that famous 'scale speed' of 130 mph, no doubt frightening the little plastic Spanish driver out of his little plastic Spanish wits.

Joining the Spanish cars were two French offerings, the Renault Alpine and Matra Jet. The Alpine series had certainly proved itself in tough long-distance rallies, as had the lesser-known

Matra, but the two Scalextric versions were based on the Le Mans cars. These had achieved some remarkable performances in the 24-hour Race, especially considering their diminutive engine sizes of 1,000 to 1100 cc for the Le Mans Matras and up to only 1300 cc for the Alpines. The two cars also look rather similar, which often causes them to be confused.

Not as confused, however, as were the motor-sport fans who first clapped eyes on two of Scalextric's other new models for 1968, the Super Javelin and Super Electra. Unlike previous Scalextric cars, these weren't based on any particular real-life counterpart but were loosely modelled on the type of sports racers that thundered round the tracks in the Can-Am racing series.

Above The cute little Spanish-built Fiat 600 appeared in 1968. The equally cute Spanish-built Abarth 850 **(top)** never made it into a UK catalogue

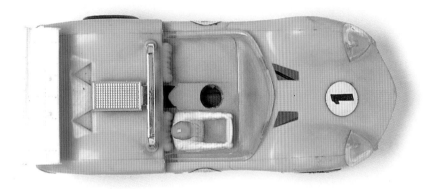

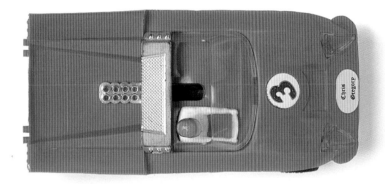

Above The Javelin and Electra models were Scalextric 'inventions'

In a similar vein, the Panther and Europa Vee models were offered as Grand Prix cars. Modelled in a Formula 1 style, the cars didn't represent any specific real-life racers but were simply examples of a 'type'.

Why produce models that don't conform to a real car that motor-sport fans will immediately recognise? There are obvious savings to be made in designing a car specifically to be manufactured in a plastic mould as opposed to trying to copy the design of an existing car and adapt it for manufacture, but inventing your own cars also means that you don't have to pay the maker of the real car a licence fee for permission to reproduce their design. Indeed, if you're looking to pick up a licence to market a model of a real car, you may well find that the manufacturer of the real car has already entered into licensing arrangements that preclude them from allowing you to produce your model. Dealing with the sponsors who have a stake in the

real car can also cause complications that are completely avoided if you invent your own car.

They may have been flights of fancy, but the Panther and Europa Vee Grand Prix Specials had been meticulously planned and came equipped with a whole new Scalextric engine/chassis combination. The 'Power Sledge' rode the track on the car's two rear wheels and the guide blade and pick-up brushes at the front. The car bodies were attached only at the rear, meaning that under acceleration the front of the body would lift, pushing more weight on to the rear wheels. On braking, the front end would sink as the weight came forward. In theory this reflected the constantly changing dynamics of a real racing car. Surging forward, the weight of a racing car transfers to the rear, giving the tyres better traction. On braking the weight comes forward to the front wheels for more accurate steering.

For the Scalextric cars, the catalogue boasted

that the new arrangement gave 'fantastic acceleration', 'tremendous speed', 'stupendous roadholding' and 'superb braking'. Power Sledge cars, it appeared, could do almost anything bar the driver getting out and making you a cup of tea at the pit stop. The arrangement worked well but was never adopted as standard across the whole range.

The Power Sledge wasn't the only major innovation for 1968, though. Up until now Scalextric models had been to a scale of 1:32 or 1:28 at most. The Super 124 series, as its name suggests, was 1:24 scale, making the cars substantially larger than Scalextric's other models.

The two basic 124 cars that came in the 124 sets were the E-type Jaguar and the Alfa Romeo GTZ. Of these the E-type is by far the better known.

Jaguar's glamour puss of the 1960s was launched at the Geneva motor show in 1961 to the same sort of reaction which had greeted Jaguar's XK120 thirteen years previously. The styling was

Below The Renault Alpine and Matra Jet gave big-hearted performances at Le Mans despite their diminutive engines

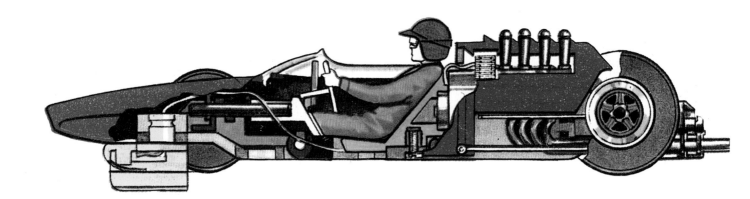

Above Catalogue cutaway showing the Super 128 Grand Prix 'Ace' cars' braking system

Below Jaguar's E-type in 1:24 scale

sensational and the car was a success from the word go. Just as the XK120 had done, the E-type won its very first race with Graham Hill driving at Oulton Park. Although no true 'factory' E-types were ever raced, the company did prepare cars for a number of different teams running E-types, including Briggs Cunningham, who took a car to

Le Mans in 1962 and brought it in in a creditable fourth place. Throughout the 1960s the special-bodied lightweight E-types were almost the only cars which could stay with the mighty Ferrari GTO on the racetrack and the Jaguar's frontline racing career would continue right up to the mid-70s.

Unlike the E-type, the Alfa Romeo GTZ was never actually intended as a production road car but was specially built by Zagato as a GT racer. In fact, its chassis and design had more in common with a Formula 1 car than with a road car. Among the car's many racing successes was a victory in the Coupe des Alpes in 1964, which was repeated the following year. Although only a few, compared with the E-type, were ever built, the GTZ is so highly prized that numerous examples still exist in racing order, still competing in classic sports car events.

The Scalextric 124 series E-type and GTZ were beautifully crafted models which were only surpassed by the 124 series Grand Prix cars, a Lotus 38 Indianapolis and a Ferrari 158.

The Lotus 38 was the car in which Jim Clark won at Indianapolis in 1965, while the Ferrari 158 helped John Surtees become World Champion in 1964 and brought Ferrari the Constructors' Cup.

The Scalextric versions featured removable drivers, magnificent glistening chrome on the

Above The 1:24 scale Alfa Romeo GTZ which partnered the E-type

Below Catalogue illustration of a Super 124 E-type passing its Scalextric rolling road test with flying colours

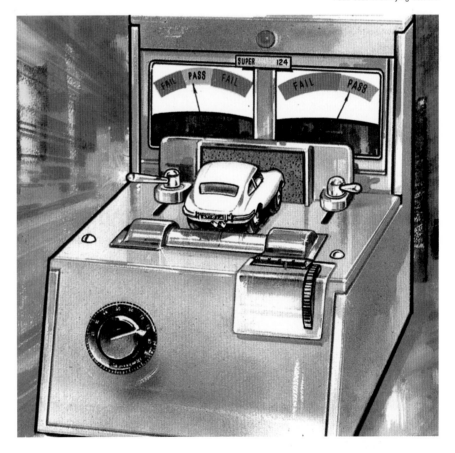

engines and exhausts and quite intricate detailing on the instrument panels. They also had what Scalextric described as 'High Hysteresis Tyres with Fine Annular Tread for Acceleration, Braking and Cornering'. High hysteresis rubber is simply rubber with less bounce, and this tyre compound was expected to help the cars deal with the higher performance that could be achieved.

The special 'ACE' versions of all four cars (the Grand Prix cars were only available as 'ACE' models) featured a front-wheel braking system with brake 'pads' which would shift forward to rub against the front wheels for greater braking power when the cars started to slow down, which is just as well, because the cars also had more powerful motors than usual. The 124 series cars had been tested at actual speeds in excess of 40 mph, meaning that you could be in charge of a vehicle exceeding the normal legal street speed limit without even having left your living room.

You'd need a pretty big living room to

accommodate a decent-sized 124 track layout, though, because, just as the cars were bigger, so was the track. There were three lanes instead of two to make it easier to double up to a six-lane race circuit. This was obviously aimed at racing clubs and the American market in particular (where 1:24 was becoming more popular anyway), but this special track was designed with stainless steel slots so that it could be built outdoors if it started to take over the house. As long as you covered it up when it rained and made sure that it was all dry before you plugged it in again, the garden was the place to be. One other drawback of the 124 system was that it needed a separate power source for each car. That meant at least two transformers for a race. Sounds expensive? It was. All of these lavish features meant that the 124 series cars were more than twice the price of the standard Scalextric models. Although it remained in production until 1970, the 124 series was perhaps not the success it deserved to be.

Back in the old, familiar small-scale 1:32 cars, new for 1969 were five Grand Prix-style cars – the Honda RA 301 as raced by John Surtees; smaller versions of the 124 series Lotus 38 and Ferrari 158; the Matra MS11 that gave the Matra Sport team its debut in Formula 1 at Monaco in 1968; and Scalextric's own Chequered Flag team car.

Far from being another 'invented' car, the Scalextric Racing Team did actually participate in motor sport, and the model is based on the Formula 3 McLaren which raced in the 1968 season. The car won its first race, although that was its only outright victory, and the chequered flag fell to terminate Scalextric's direct involvement in real motor racing at the end of that season.

To add to that package, Scalextric had four new GT cars to expand their range of exotic sports racers, including the Ford 200 GT, the Ford-Mirage, and two cars that have each been described as the most beautiful sports car ever made, the

The Russian-built Miura **(left)** was no match for the UK version **(right)**

Lambourghini Miura and the Ferrari P4.

The Ferrari was a purpose-built racing car designed for prototype and endurance racing. Its 4-litre V12 engine could take it from a standing start to 60 mph in around 5 seconds and on up to 200 mph. Two P4s ran second and third to the 7-litre Ford at Le Mans in 1967, although the P4 won Ferrari the overall prototype championship that year, beating Porsche by just 2 points.

While the swoops and curves of the P4 are clearly the garb of a racing car and could never really

when you're driving a car as fantastic as this on the road, you want to go slowly enough to be seen in it, don't you?

Despite the introduction of new models and new gimmicks, business was now not quite so buoyant at Scalextric. Sales were in decline and the heavy investment that had gone into new lines such as the 124 series meant that something of a crisis was developing. To be fair, other manufacturers of slot car racing systems were also suffering, perhaps because there was now such great and diverse

be mistaken for a road car, the Lamborghini Miura's elegant styling slips easily between both worlds. Primarily, of course, the car was intended as an exotic road car. Like the Ferrari, it had a massive V12 engine and, also like the Ferrari, it could hit 60 mph quicker than you could write out a cheque for the petrol. The top speed was a little down on the Ferrari's at only just over 170 mph, but let's face it,

competition in the toy market.

By 1969, Action Man had been around in the UK for three years and GI Joe in America (the inspiration for Action Man) for even longer. The soldier dolls had a range of working equipment that included a deep-sea diver's outfit in which you could make your Action Man descend into the depths of a pond (or the bath) and rise to the surface again. He had a mortar that actually fired bombs, a bazooka that actually fired shells and a flame thrower that . . . well, it didn't actually do anything but it looked the business. He also had his own jeep, armoured car, armoured personnel carrier and spaceship. Stiff competition in the area of imaginative play.

On the model car front, competition was even greater. Corgi's version of James Bond's Aston Martin had a working ejector seat, pop-up bulletproof screen and pop-out machine guns and battering rams. It was available in October 1965 (two years before the Scalextric version), well in time for Christmas and when the movie was still fresh in people's minds. It sold almost 4 million in this original version and became the toy that everyone had to have that year, selling out in the UK faster than the shops could get it on the shelves.

Corgi followed up the Bond phenomenon with John Steed's Bentley and Emma Peel's Lotus as seen in *The Avengers* TV series; a *Man From Uncle* Oldsmobile where you could press down the rear-view periscope on the roof and watch Ilya Kuriakin and Napoleon Solo alternately pop out of the left and right windows to fire their guns; and best of all, in 1966 they gave the world the Batmobile, with a pop-out circular saw on the front and a working rocket launcher.

What could possibly be more exciting than that, except perhaps *Thunderbirds*' Lady Penelope's Pink 'FAB 1' Rolls-Royce that fired a rocket from behind

Below The Matra MS11 came with enough pipework to re-plumb your bathroom

Below The Ferrari P4, 1967 world
sports prototype championship winner

the famous Rolls-Royce radiator grill, or the
big green Thunderbird 2 which dropped a pod
containing the little yellow Thunderbird 4 – all
available from Dinky Toys?

The hard core of Scalextric racing fans were,
of course, unaffected by such juvenile diversions,
but competition for children's attention, and pocket
money, was never tougher and a long hard look
at the Scalextric range would have to be
taken as the company moved forward into
a new decade.

Left Final catalogue of the Sixties
gave the reader a rear-view mirror
perspective of Formula 1, or the
last thing you'd see before you
were run over

Extra Bits for Added Fun

Right The Scalextric buildings were modelled on the real thing at Goodwood

Let's face it, for car nuts the sight of an exotic sports car or dynamic racer is enough to bring on palpitations, and the smell of a warm V12 or the burble of a barely silenced V8 can leave even the hulking hairiest of petrolheads moved to tears. The cars, then, are the big attraction for the vast majority of Scalextric fans, and the track and accessories are just things you need to make the cars go. But that's not all there is to it.

We must never forget that Scalextric racing takes place as much in your head as it does on the track. The cars are modelled, for the most part, on real racers and have always incorporated as much detail as the manufacturing process would allow to make them look as true to their full-size counterparts as possible. Why? Because a model that looks right turns the key that fires up the imagination. Then, after a couple of laps' competitive racing against another 'driver', adrenalin kicks in like a cerebral turbo and you're there in the

Below Six possible layouts for the 1960 sets

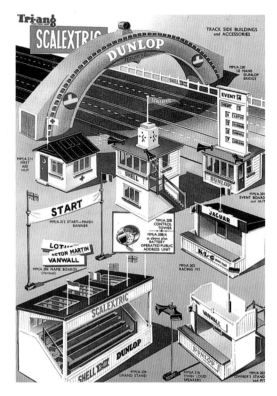

car lapping Hockenheim or the Brickyard in the race of your life. On the other hand, maybe I should switch to decaf.

The cars, naturally, have to look the part. That's what makes Scalextric such enormous fun. What on earth would be the point in racing a shapeless blob of plastic around a track? Given that so much attention to detail goes into the cars, it follows that anything which enhances their image will help to fuel the imagination and add to the fun. That's where the accessories that have been available over the years, many modelled every bit as accurately as the cars themselves, come into their own.

Naturally, there are practical considerations to be taken into account as well, not least with the track. The actual design of the track hasn't changed much since the very beginning. The early track slotted together, the guide rails fitting inside one

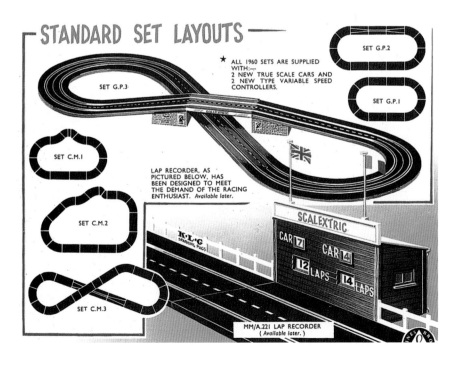

another, and could be secured underneath with small clips. It was a fragile system, though, and the electrical contact between the rails could be lost as the ends became worn from regular assembling and dismantling. The actual track was made from rubber and had an annoying tendency to warp.

All of that changed in 1963 with the introduction of the new 'Flexible and Virtually Unbreakable' Plexytrack. The Plexytrack name had been used since the late Fifties, but the all-new Plexytrack was made from warp-free polyethylene and had connectors built in at each end – essentially the same track that is used today.

At the advent of the plastic car era in 1960, there were over a dozen different pieces of track available, some of which appeared to be designed to encourage the complete destruction of your cars. The Humpback Bridge would send your Vanwall into orbit if you took it too fast and the 'chicane' brought both slots together, providing an ideal opportunity for ramming, shoulder-charging and general mayhem. The 'cross-over', however, afforded the perfect opportunity for maximum high-speed contact. Here the tracks crossed at right angles, like a traffic junction without the traffic lights. If the two cars were heading for the cross-over from different directions, you had three options: go headlong for the junction and hope you

made it first, swallow your pride and ease off to let your rival through first, or go for the big hit and hope you survived the carnage. See? Accessories can be fun, too!

By the time the plastic Vanwall and Lotus were available, there was also a range of trackside buildings to add an even more authentic touch to your layout. The Le Mans Dunlop Bridge provided a scenic arch under which the cars passed, but most of the buildings were modelled on the real thing at the Goodwood circuit, which was quite close to Scalextric's Havant factory. Among the range of buildings was a grandstand, a first-aid hut and a control tower with a battery-operated public address system with little speakers and a microphone so that you could let your entire circuit know that Mum had decided it was bath time.

More accessories were added each year, including, in 1962, a café (oh, if only the drivers had

Above The famous Le Mans Dunlop Bridge

Above A not-so-famous humpback bridge

Below 1961's Grande Bridge playing host to two Ferrari GTOs
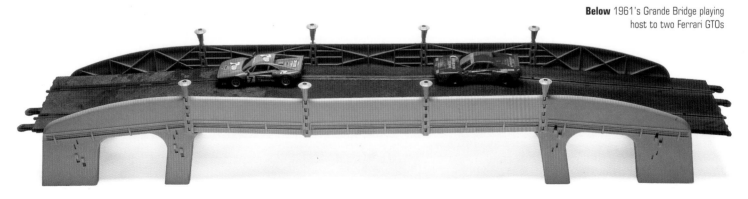

53

hands to hold a cup of tea and a bacon sandwich) and a manually operated lap counter. You pressed a button on the roof to register another lap on the scoreboard each time you passed – the correct button for your track, otherwise you were giving the race away. There was a TV crew in a scaffolding tower to film the impressive new Le Mans start track sections (oh, if only the drivers had legs to run across the track to their cars) or the Goodwood Chicane section. A couple of kinks had been added at the entrance and exit to a converging slot section with hay bales, bushes and oil drums to be scattered by the skidding cars. Authentic injuries could be sustained if you knelt on one of those little oil drums when you were crawling across the floor to put your car back on the track (oh, if only the track marshals weren't just lifeless little plastic figures).

A major part of the fun of Scalextric has always been designing your own track layout and making it all fit with the pieces you have available. It could become very frustrating if you devised a route that would take you into the dark under the sideboard (great to watch the new cars with real lights coming blazing out of the darkness) but you then realised

Right Once you had painted your spectators, they could be safely seated in the grandstand

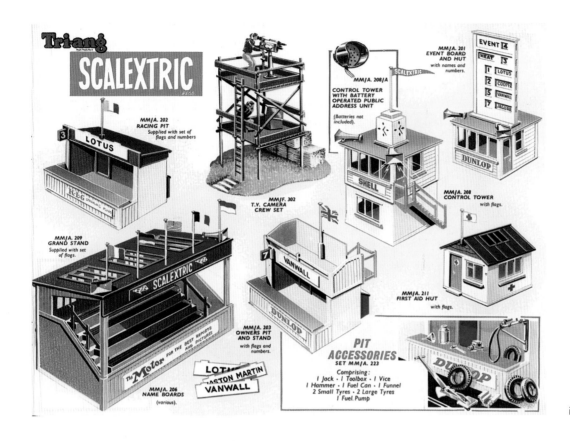

Left Prior to the introduction of photographs in the catalogue, the illustrations had a charm all of their own

that you didn't have enough track to make it back to the start and complete the circuit. The 1961 catalogue offered a partial solution in the Race Track Folder, which included diagrams showing how to build 'Many exciting 2 and 4 lane circuits including some designed on world famous race tracks . . .'

You couldn't miss the end of the race when the battery-operated Timekeeper's Hut became available in 1962. It featured an electric countdown hooter to let you know when to wave the chequered flag, although by the following year you might not make it to the end of the race, even if you had managed to keep your car on the track for the full distance. The Fuel Load Gauge meddled with the power being delivered to your car to simulate the effect of running with a full tank of fuel, making the car run slightly slower at the start of a race and then

gradually pick up pace as it lightened its load until the tank was finally empty and you ground to a halt!

Sadly, the Fuel Load Gauge wasn't synchronised to the 45 rpm extended play sound effects record which you could stick on your Dansette to listen to a start signal, the thunder of real racing engines and a finish signal for four different Grand Prix and Tourist Trophy races. Surely now even the most hard-hearted, cynical petrolhead must have been in gasoline Valhalla.

A range of DIY self-assembly building kits that helped to cut the cost of construction around your Scalextric set from 1963 onwards might have left some pocket money for the new electrically controlled lap recorder in 1964. Now you no longer had to worry about hitting the wrong button and awarding unraced laps to your adversary.

Below 1962's manually operated lap counter

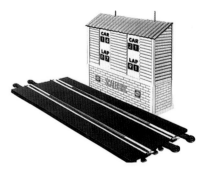

By 1965 the range of Scalextric extras available was vast. There was decorative freestanding fencing quite separate from the regular crash barriers you could fix to the track, as well as enough building options to establish your own village. A variety of track supports designed to create banking on the track and allow you to lap faster (and in the dark as track lighting had been available since 1962) could be wedged under an ever-increasing choice of track sections. New track features included a tricky little skid chicane and an elaborate hillclimb or dragster loop which could be used for sprint racing quite separately from a normal circuit.

And yet there was more – more danger, more realism and most of all, more noise. A battery-operated penalty buzzer skid chicane sounded the alert if your swerving car nudged one of the oil-drum sensors, and Dad's post-lunch Sunday afternoon armchair snooze was unlikely to survive the din from the Twin Auto Screams. This neat device was attached to your hand control to provide an authentic engine noise with rising decibels tuned to the rising speed of the car and, doubtless, the boiling rage of your luckless father.

Spare parts were now extensively available for Scalextric cars, which was just as well, because there were now even more ways to cause serious damage. The Change Over Track had you and your opponent cross over onto each other's tracks. This meant that on a simple loop circuit, the car on the inside didn't always have the advantage of the shorter track on corners. The change-over sections were used in pairs, so that you crossed back onto your own track again, manufacturing yet another opportunity for a major fender-bender.

Blow Out gave another taste of destruction in the form of a simulated high-speed tyre failure. The difference between this and real tyre failure was that you could make your opponent crash. The device was a humpback bridge section which incorporated a paddle buried in the track. Using skill, judgement, cunning and malice, you pressed a button on your hand control just as the rival car's front wheel hit the paddle and up it flipped. An

instant later your opponent would find his Ferrari parked upside down in the café, ending his race and ruining the Eccles cakes.

Yet another kind of lap counter also came into play in 1966, this time set into the track and operated physically by the cars as they passed over the special track section. Of course, if you'd just

Also, if you had driven an intelligent and skilful race, remembered that the cars will slow down for corners as well as speed up along the straights, and survived all the pitfalls to come out victorious, you could now be awarded a tiny Scalextric driver-sized laurel wreath or silver trophy. Okay, so that was for your driver. You could proudly wear an enamel

been totalled in the Blow Out, notching up another lap was the least of your problems.

As if you didn't have enough to do with your hands in keeping your car on the track, blasting up the revs for the Auto Scream or giving your opposite number flying lessons on the Blow Out, yet another hand control feature was now available which 'switched the points' on the track, rather as if on a railway system, allowing you to drive into a special pit lane to have a word with your mechanics about that strange knocking noise coming from your front suspension. Previously the pit-lane control had been via a small button on the track, so this really was a useful innovation.

Left The Race Folder grew into a 101 circuit booklet

Below This scaffold for the use of the TV crew was available from 1961

Right The starter on this rostrum has lost his flag at some point over the last 40 years. Most of the spectators and pit crew are keen to help find it, although the driver fourth from right would obviously rather just relax with the cigarette in his right hand

Scalextric badge with a chequered flag motif to let everyone know you were World Champion in your street.

There was always the next race to face, though, and a new circuit to master. The Scalextric Race Folder had now been expanded to offer no fewer than 101 different circuits which could be built with the track sections now available. As part of each one, you could build in 1968's electric lap counter (yes, another one!), which was activated by the cars as they passed over its special track section and

could record up to an exhausting, thumb-numbing 999 laps.

The year 1969 saw the introduction of a new element of track in the High Hump Bridge, which could act like a launching ramp if you didn't time your braking just right. Even if you didn't take off at the top, the car was hard to keep under control as the steep incline and swift descent jolted it back and forward. Had your driver been able to eat a bacon sandwich in the café before your rival destroyed it after the Blow Out, the High Hump Bridge is where he would have lost it.

The 'High Hump Bridge' sometimes seemed a bit like a launching ramp, but the Flying Leap really was one! The scenario is simple to imagine. You're racing towards a bridge over a fast-flowing river when suddenly you realise that the bridge has been

Right You could buy miniature winners' trophies for your lucky drivers

Right Twin Auto Screams gave you mayhem on tap

58

washed away. It's too late to do anything else but, you guessed it, leap the gap. Special embossed sections helped to guide the car back into its slot on the other side of the leap, but if you were going too slowly you wouldn't make it over; too fast and you could overshoot the guides.

The accessories available from Scalextric in the Sixties added hugely to the enjoyment of model motor racing both for the growing number of 'serious' club racers as well as the living-room champions, and there would be yet more innovations to come in the 1970s.

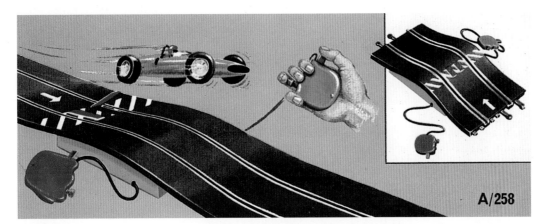

A/258

Left Blow Out provided the opportunity to launch your opponent into orbit

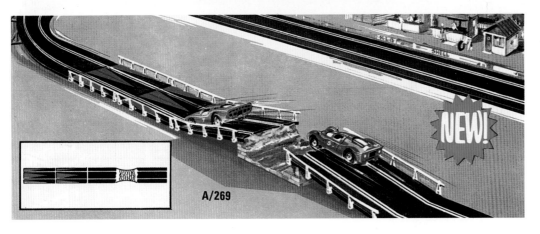

A/269

Left In 1969 the first of many versions of the Flying Leap appeared

Twists and
Turns in
Troubled
Times

Twists and Turns in Troubled Times

Right The 1970 catalogue. Scalextric racing looked just like this . . . if you were a spaced-out hippie

The new decade dawned on a world fascinated by all things big and small. One of the biggest things ever, man landing on the moon, had happened the previous summer, and you could now step boldly out in your biggest flared trousers to buy Britain's biggest new car, the Range Rover, while totting up the bill on your incredibly small new pocket calculator.

For fans of small-scale motoring, Scalextric, ever keen to stay one jump ahead of the competition with an innovative new product, introduced You Steer cars. The ingenious steering system worked via a pivoting arm beneath the car which moved the car sideways in relation to the track slot (the guide blade, of course, remained in the slot), allowing the car to skid round corners or, more specifically, around a range of obstacles that could be placed on the track. You Steered using a steering wheel attached to your hand control which activated the mechanism. Response from the car was instant and, as the 1970 catalogue put it, this was 'the fantastic new development that makes the most of your skill'.

Scalextric boasted that 'You Steer gives you instant response for surging round the tightest bends, positive overtaking, and manoeuvring round obstacles' and the system did indeed add a whole new dimension to Scalextric racing. Using the system effectively, though, was a difficult art to master. You had to use both hands, for a start, meaning that you no longer had one hand free to sling the cat out of the way when it decided to take a nap in the middle of the Mulsanne Straight. Similarly, you no longer had a free hand to keep yourself supplied with the Jaffa Cakes so essential for sustenance during lengthy endurance races.

There was no doubt, however, that You Steer added to the fun of Scalextric racing but it was never really as popular with Scalextric fans as it deserved to be. It was destined to stay in production for only two years, financial difficulties within the Scalextric organisation ultimately providing the obstacle that it couldn't quite manage to slither round.

The heavy investment in You Steer meant that new cars for 1970 were limited to the 'Formula 1-style' Dart GP and the wedge-shaped sports prototype 'Can-Am-style' Cougar Sports, neither of which did much to fire the imaginations of Scalextric enthusiasts.

Sneaking onto the back pages of the 1970 catalogue, and kept totally separate from the motor-racing range, was the weird and wonderful Jump Jockey outfit. This horse-racing circuit ran on its own plastic track with fragile little horses on sticks, looking rather like the horses on fairground rides, whizzing round a green plastic track. The jockeys were so small they made Frankie Dettori look like Arnold Schwarzenegger. Their electric power was supplied to tiny sled affairs which ran below the 'turf'. The whole rig took so long to set up that by the time you were ready to race, the horses would only have been fit for the knacker's yard (or, in France, the à la carte menu). Keeping Jump Jockey strictly separate from the real business of model motor racing was a wise move.

Other moves were also afoot. The boom years of the 1960s were over and the entire toy trade was facing a recession. Scalextric suffered along with everyone else, and the company changed hands, eventually ending up as part of Rovex, now Hornby Hobbies Ltd. Production at the Havant factory ceased and manufacture of Scalextric was transferred to the Hornby/Rovex plant in Margate, Kent.

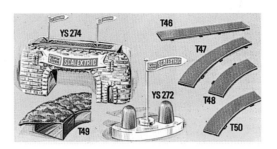

Left A number of new hazards were introduced for You Steer cars to negotiate as well as track borders to keep their rear ends on the plastic

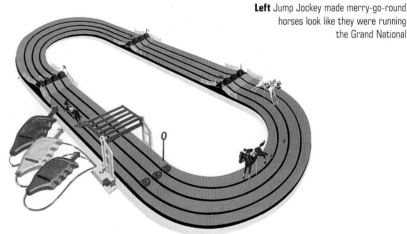

Left Jump Jockey made merry-go-round horses look like they were running the Grand National

Below The Scalextric Ford-Mirage was a true endurance racer lasting from 1969 through to 1974

The move and the financial constraints dictated that only five new cars appeared in the 1971 catalogue, one of which was a simple update (a 'wing' had been added in line with current trends in Grand Prix design) of the Scalextric Team Car.

The Scalletti-Arrow was also offered as a Grand Prix/Indy car type of single-seat racer but Scalextric weren't fooling anyone with this exotically named hybrid, which was clearly just the old Dart GP with a rear wing and a different chrome engine stuck on the back. Of far more interest to Formula 1 fans was the third new single-seat model, the BRM 83 as driven by Jackie Stewart.

Stewart had a sensational year in 1971. He became World Champion for the second time (his first was in 1969) and also competed in the Can-Am series, where he won a couple of races. His World Championships had come at the wheel of a Tyrrell, however, not a BRM. Stewart raced the BRM 83 in 1966 and 67, although he didn't fare too well with it. The car's complicated and over-ambitious 'H 16' engine configuration, basically two 8-cylinder engines in one unit, was highly temperamental, and its unreliability proved to be its undoing. Thankfully, there were no such problems with the Spanish-built Scalextric version.

Despite the heavy dark clouds of recession, the hazy blue-grey clouds of exhaust fumes continued to blossom above motor-racing circuits around the world. Going racing was an increasingly expensive business for major car manufacturers, and racing teams now relied ever more heavily on sponsorship to survive. None of this detracted from the glamour of the sport, though. In fact, the big money involved gave motor sport an even greater appeal. Movie idol petrolheads Paul Newman and Steve McQueen certainly helped boost the starry image of motor sport; both raced cars themselves and both starred in motor-racing films. Newman's race drama *Winning*, in which his wife also starred, had been released in 1969 and McQueen's lovingly made, if somewhat self-indulgent, *Le Mans* came in 1971.

There could not have been a better time, therefore, to introduce the Scalextric Porsche 917 GT, appropriately enough – for a car which covered itself in glory at Le Mans – manufactured in France.

The real Porsche 917 started life in 1968 as a project aimed at providing Porsche with an unbeatable contender in the World Sports Car Championship. The car was designed, built and ready for its inaugural races in 1969. Such was the power developed by its 4.5-litre flat-12 engine that the 917 hit speeds approaching 230 mph at Le Mans, the car going like a rocket and tending to try to emulate one, too. Given the chance, the 917 would take to the air, and keeping it on the road became something of a problem for the drivers. Sadly, private entrant John Woolf was killed when his 917 crashed out of control at Le Mans that year.

It was all different the next year, though. The aerodynamics problems were overcome and the 917 really got into its stride, with Porsche taking first, second and third place at Le Mans, albeit that third place went to a Porsche 908, not a 917. In fact, the 917 completely dominated the World Sports Car Championship, with the first Gulf Porsche 917 in its distinctive blue and orange livery notching up notable wins in the Daytona 24 Hours and at Watkins Glen in America, although they suffered

Left Someone must really have liked the 1969 catalogue, because the artwork was revised for 1971

Left The Scalextric Ford 3L trying to steal the limelight from the Porsche 917

Left The March Ford displaying its tea-tray front wing in real life and in Scalextric form on the cover of the 1972 catalogue. Photography was used on the cover for the first time on this issue

mechanical problems at Sebring (where Steve McQueen came second in a 908).

In 1971, the 917 again took first and second place at Le Mans ahead of three Ferraris, with the Italians ending up in something of a German sandwich, being followed by more Porsches than you could shake a bratwurst at. Remarkably, the next eight finishers in the race were all Porsches, making this Porsche's finest Le Mans performance to date (they would go on to better it in the 1980s). It was definitely the moment to introduce a Scalextric 917.

The final Scalextric offering for 1971 was a dear old friend, the Jaguar E-type. Jaguar's style icon of the Sixties was now fully ten years old, but it was still in production and would remain so for another three years. The latest E-type was powered by Jaguar's fabulous 5.3-litre V12 engine, which sent the big cat roaring up to 60 mph in around 6.5 seconds and gave it a top speed of just a whisker under 150 mph.

In 1970, around 70 per cent of all Jaguars sold in the United States were E-types, and the car was still extremely competitive on the racetrack. The new V12 made sure that it stayed in contention right up to the end of its frontline racing career, with Bob Tullius's Group 44 team victorious in their modified E-type in 1975 at Sports Car Club of America races in St Louis, Summit Point, Brainerd, Nelson Ledges, Lime Rock, Indianapolis and at the finals at Road Atlanta, where they became National Champions.

Scalextric had produced an E-type before, of course, with the big 1:24 scale car, but this was the first time that the Jaguar had been manufactured in the standard scale size.

13th edition

SCALEXTRIC

Model Motor Racing

New exciting sets you can always add to

Right Big cat and little kitten, the 1:24 and 1:32 Jaguar E-types

Left The Auto Union and Alfa Romeo models made a surprise reappearance in the 1971 catalogue having been unavailable for a couple of years

Experimental Races

The glittering excesses of glam rock held Britain in a sequinned stranglehold in 1972, Marc Bolan's T Rex topping the UK singles chart with 'Telegram Sam', later to be followed by 'Metal Guru'. Slade were also making huge strides in their preposterously platformed shoes, hitting the No.1 spot with 'Take Me Bak 'Ome and 'Mama Weer All Crazee Now', while in New York the musical *Grease* enjoyed its début performance.

The bizarre style explosion in the Seventies would have passed by anyone who had been stuck in the loft since 1966 building the ultimate home racetrack layout, but youngsters with more modest Scalextric sets could enjoy the spectacle of their elder sister's boyfriend lowering himself down to floor level to join in the race and then destroying the entire circuit when he fell flat on his face as he tried to stand up again with the massive heels of his platform shoes caught in the backs of his outrageously flared trousers.

The rest of the world may have been going a bit bananas, but Scalextric was still smarting slightly from the recent setbacks it had endured, and there were only four new models on offer in 1972.

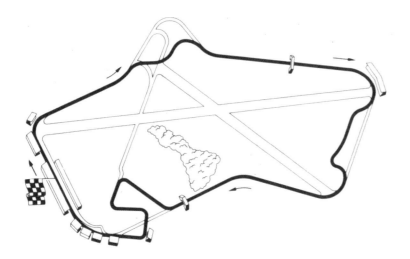

Above Silverstone, venue for the McLaren M9A's only Formula 1 appearance, could be accurately reproduced in Scalextric form

For Formula 1 fans, there were the 'March Ford 721' and the 'McLaren F1'.

Scalextric's March was billed in the catalogue as being 'based on the car that finished in the money throughout the 1971 Grand Prix season', although later catalogues would describe it as being the car that raced in the South African Grand Prix in 1972 or the Argentinian Grand Prix of the same year. In fact, the distinctive rounded tray-shaped wing and rounded nose point to it being based on the March 711 as driven by Ronnie Peterson in 1971. An interim car designated 721 did appear in South Africa and Argentina before the completely new 721X and G cars were ready to race in 1972. The giveaway is in the numbered designations – 711 was the 1971 car and 721 denoted a 1972 March.

None of the above catastrophe of confusion made any difference whatsoever to swimmer Mark Spitz, who headed home for America from the 1972 Olympic Games in Munich wearing so many gold medals that he could hardly stand upright (he won seven). Neither should it make any difference

to anyone else. The fact was that Scalextric had a new Grand Prix model based on a state-of-the-art (well, only a year out of date) car that looked like it really meant business. The front and rear wings were the sort of features that lit the blue touchpaper on the firecracker imaginations of Scalextric racers. Fun beats number-crunching any day.

The other Grand Prix car was announced as 'The McLaren F1' and was based on the McLaren M9A (there we go with those numbers again!). The car was notable, but not for its racing success. It only ever competed in one Grand Prix, at Silverstone in 1969. It was never competitive and retired with suspension failure. So why is it notable? It had four-wheel drive, something that was seen as being the way forward for Formula 1 in the late Sixties. A number of different constructors, including Lotus and Matra as well as McLaren, experimented with four-wheel drive but it was never a success. The advantages of traction that were theoretically gained on the racetrack by having the power transmitted to the tarmac via four wheels instead of two were outweighed, quite literally, by the extra weight required for the four-wheel drive system. Technical advances in body and wing design which provided enough downforce to give traditional cars better traction, also contributed to the downfall of the four-wheel-drive revolution.

The Scalextric version, of course, had two-wheel drive anyway. The other two newcomers for 1972 were the 'Ferrari 330 GT' and the Wankel Mercedes.

The Ferrari should not be confused with the rather elegant, mid-Sixties four seat 330 GT road car. In fact, what Scalextric were now calling the 330 GT was actually an open-topped version of the P4 that they had first introduced in 1969.

Alongside the Ferrari was the Mercedes Wankel C111. Looking every bit the GT racer, with 'gull-wing' doors and styling that made it appear as though it had been designed for a futuristic TV series – in fact Ed Straker's car in the Gerry Anderson TV sci-fi series *UFO* was rather reminiscent of the C111 – the Mercedes seemed to be the car to watch out for on the racetrack. You'd still be watching out now, though, if you wanted to see a real C111 going racing. The only place it's ever been pitted against rival cars has been on the Scalextric track. The real car never raced.

and produce more noxious exhaust fumes than a normal motor. Mercedes eventually abandoned their Wankel programme without ever having put the engine into production, although Japanese manufacturer Mazda persevered with their version, which powered their incredibly successful RX-7 sports cars.

The C111 was never produced in serious numbers and, although the rotary engine could whisk it up to 60 mph in just 4.8 seconds and on with turbine smoothness up to almost 190 mph, the car's biggest rival on the track would have been

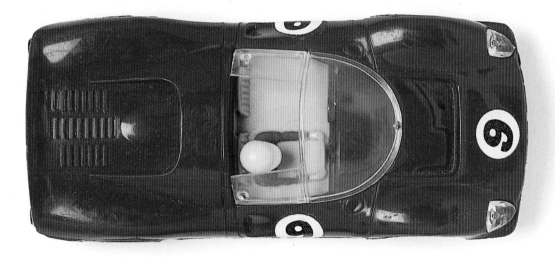

Right Ferrari 330 GT – a P4 for drivers who liked to feel the sun on their helmets

What it did was to act as a testbed and publicity vehicle for Daimler-Benz. The reason that it attracted so much publicity was that it was powered by a version of the Wankel rotary engine developed under licence by Daimler-Benz. This engine was unusual in that instead of having pistons that pumped up and down to turn a drive shaft that turned the wheels, it had an engine that spun round, giving a smoother transfer of power to the drive shaft. Although they produced less noise and vibration, Wankel engines did tend to use more fuel

the all-conquering Porsche 917, against which it wouldn't have stood much of a chance.

A final version of the C111 was produced in 1973 when a mothballed car was brought out of hibernation and fitted with a more conventional diesel engine. It went on to break numerous speed and endurance records, all the while promoting Daimler-Benz's diesel engines.

Along with the Ferrari and the McLaren, Scalextric's Mercedes C111 was produced in Spain.

Porsche Spice

The big Scalextric news for 1973 came in the foreword to the new catalogue. A special section of 'High Speed Banked Track' had been introduced that now allowed you to 'lap the circuit at scale speeds of up to 200 mph'. The scale speed of 130 mph was now as out of date as miniskirts and hot pants, and half a dozen new cars were listed to help you reach the magical 200 mph.

The Ferrari 312B2 was fielded by the Maranello team in 1971 and 1972, winning the Dutch Grand Prix in 71 and the German Grand Prix in 72 at the hands of Belgian driver Jacky Ickx. The strange streamlined cowl which ran from behind the driver's head up onto the rear wing of the car had the look of a Ku-Klux-Klan-hood but wasn't nearly as bizarre as the bulky nose section added to the car (not in the Scalextric version) for the South African Grand Prix

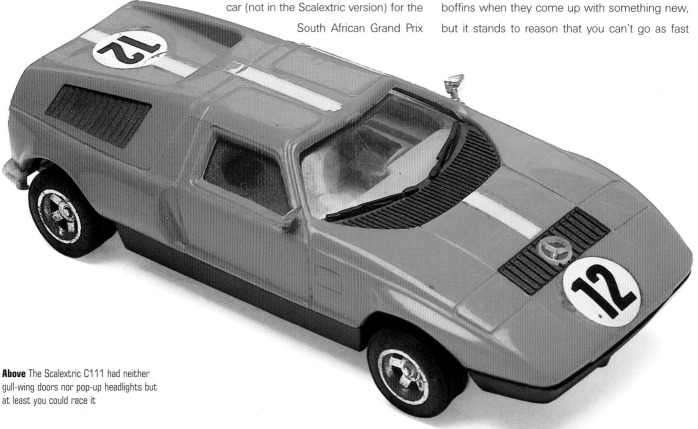

at Kyalami. The weird new front wing made the car look like a hammerhead shark but did not give it the higher top speed that wind tunnel tests had promised. You have to listen to the wind tunnel boffins when they come up with something new, but it stands to reason that you can't go as fast

Above The Scalextric C111 had neither gull-wing doors nor pop-up headlights but at least you could race it

SCALEXTRIC
Model
Motor
Racing

1968, almost all of their cars, with a few notable exceptions, having had Ford power.

In 1972, Emerson Fittipaldi did for Lotus what Stewart had done for Tyrrell the previous year. He won the World Championship and the Constructors' Cup in a car powered by the Ford-Cosworth. The Scalextric Lotus 72 was a stunning rendition of Fittipaldi's car, resplendent in the black and gold livery of Lotus's sponsors, John Player Special. The Lotus 72 was the first of the famous JPS cars, but the gold detailing on the real car wasn't actually gold at all. It was more of a dull beige colour, deliberately painted that way so that it would come out looking gold when the car was photographed or seen on TV. Shiny gold graphics would reflect too much light and could appear in photos or on telly as white or grey or even disappear altogether.

The sponsorship deal also required the team's name to be changed to John Player Special Team Lotus, as Imperial Tobacco, who produced John Player Special cigarettes, were craftily trying to dodge what they thought might be an imminent ban on cigarette advertising. They believed that if legislation was introduced to stop them from advertising directly, they would still be able to plug their product every time the team was mentioned.

The Scalextric JPS Lotus did have shiny gold detailing and was a very well-received addition to any fan's collection.

Ready to scare the sauerkraut out of the Mercedes C111 was the Scalextric Porsche 917K. The 'K' stood for 'kurz', which means 'short' in German and identifies the shorter variant of the 917. Why shorten it? The idea came from an English engineer, John Horsman, who prepared cars for the Gulf team. He believed that shortening the car would help to solve its handling problems and make

when you're carrying something the size of a bookcase on your nose. Any hammerhead shark could have told you that.

These weren't exactly glory years for Ferrari, who by 1973 hadn't won the Constructors' Championship or produced a World Champion driver for ten years. All that would start to change the following year with a brand-new car and the arrival of Niki Lauda.

Scalextric still had a few aces up their sleeve for 1973, though, with a slightly revised version of the March Ford 721 cropping up and a Tyrrell Ford based on the car in which Jackie Stewart became the 1971 World Champion and won Tyrrell the Constructors' Cup. The helmet into which Stewart squeezed his shoulder-length hair and knee-length sideburns sat in front of a Ford-Cosworth V8 engine. Numerous racing teams used the Ford-Cosworth unit and Tyrrell's association with the company goes back to their first foray into Formula 1 in

it even faster. He was right. Porsche subsequently tried a number of different tail-end treatments on the 917 and the beast just went from strength to strength.

The final new car for 1973 was a pretty little model which was manufactured in France and only officially available in the UK for one year, although it was around for much longer in France. The Scalextric Renault Alpine was based on the Alpine A310, unveiled at the Geneva motor show in 1971 and trading on the racing success of the old Alpine A110, but intended more as a luxury sports car for everyday use than an out-and-out racer. The first cars didn't race in earnest until 1974 and they proved a little too cumbersome for their 1800 cc engines, the lack of power meaning that the A310 was never quite able to match up to the successes of its more nimble predecessor. The A310 was far more at home as a boulevard cruiser than storming up a mountain track. Just like the Scalextric Mercedes Wankel C111, though, on the slotted track it's every bit as good as the next car and it has the styling to look like a winner even if the real car was a bit of a sheep in wolf's clothing. Later versions of the road car had a 2.6-litre V6 engine which gave significant improvements in performance.

Sales of high-performance cars were, however, suffering hugely in the wake of the oil crisis that erupted in 1973, causing the price of oil to soar by 70 per cent. You could always adopt an alternative means of transport, as the skateboard craze was flourishing. In the UK, you would have had plenty of time to grab some air on your board while practising your '4 Out Block' and flipping 'Ollies' on the pavement as 1974 came round,

because the economic crisis and oil shortages had led to the famous three-day working week. Maybe that's what enticed Russian ballet dancer Mikhail Baryshnikov to defect in Toronto. He obviously wanted to head for London, where nobody had to work more than three days and he could show those skateboarders a few mean moves while queuing outside Britain's first McDonald's restaurant and listening to Abba's monster hit 'Waterloo'. Or maybe not.

In the midst of a depression, much of it surely caused by 'Waterloo', Scalextric could muster only three new models for 1974, and one of them wasn't actually new at all.

The Tiger Special was a Can-Am style car that looked remarkably like the old Electra with a new rear wing and some fancy decoration. That's probably because it was the old Electra with a new

Right The JPS Lotus looked extremely impressive in black and gold – certainly not dull beige

rear wing and some fancy decoration. If you're now starting to think that Scalextric were constantly trying to pull the wool over their customers' eyes by presenting tarted-up old models as new cars, then stop for a while and consider how real racing cars evolve. Completely new cars don't appear every season but the new season's car will often incorporate developments which leave it looking much like its predecessor, albeit with modifications. Why shouldn't Scalextric model motor-racing cars follow the same pattern?

The two brand-new cars for 1974 were, in any case, of far greater interest.

Mexico or Bust

The Shadow team had been founded in 1968 and spent a couple of seasons racing in the Can-Am Challenge before graduating to Formula 1 in 1973. The Scalextric Shadow was based on the DN1

Above Another version of the JPS Lotus. Later Scalextric cars would drop the JPS cigarette advertising

which first competed in the South African Grand Prix, where it was driven by the American George Follmer, who had won the 1972 Can-Am Challenge for Porsche, and Jackie Oliver, who had driven in Can-Am for Shadow.

The Shadow cars would compete in Formula 1 up to 1980 with only minor successes to keep their spirits up. Too often, it seemed, they really were just shadows. The same could not be said of Scalextric's other new car for 1974, the Ford Escort Mexico.

The Mexico was derived from Ford's incredibly successful Mark 1 Escort Twin Cam rally car. This was the car that almost turned certain rally events into one-make races such was the popularity of the Escort among private entrants. The Ford factory teams, of course, were the leaders of the pack. Even the amazing Mini didn't see as much rally

Left The 1974 catalogue appeared to show Scalextric drivers living out their fantasies by racing on a real circuit

Right The 1975 catalogue with the JPS Lotus. Was that really dull beige?

Below The Shadow Formula 1 car received a facelift in 1976 and appeared in this, its final guise, in 1980

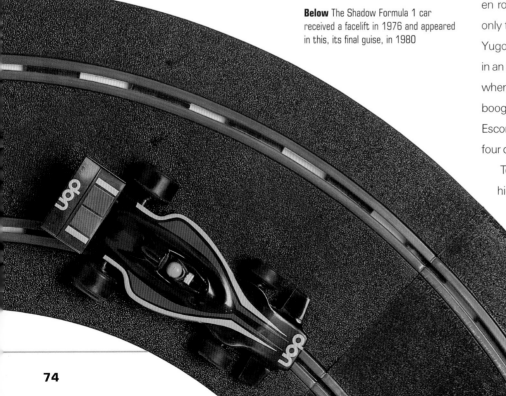

action in as many different kinds of rally as the cheeky little Ford.

The Escort first raced in 1968 in the San Remo Rally, where it finished third, returning home in time to have a few problems ironed out before Rally supremo Roger Clark notched up the car's first victory in the Circuit of Ireland later that year. Escorts would go on to win the Tulip Rally, the Austrian Alpine, the Acropolis Rally and the 1000 Lakes Rally, all in 1968.

The Mk 1 Escort in all its various forms quickly became the dominant force in international rally events, with fierce competition coming from the likes of the Porsche 911, right up to 1975 when the Mark II Escort took over.

The Escort Mexico variant came about as a tribute to the Ford team's immense victory in the 1970 London–Mexico Marathon. The race involved a tour of Europe prior to crossing the Atlantic and a tour of South America ending up in Mexico City. Special stages to test the cars to the limit were thrown in en route. Seven Escorts were entered by Ford and only two failed to finish, the first casualty coming in Yugoslavia, where Colin Malkin's car came off worst in an argument with a truck. The second was in Brazil, when Roger Clark's car danced the fender-bender boogie with a VW Beetle. Hannu Mikola took his Escort to first place in Mexico City and the remaining four cars finished third, fifth, sixth and eighth.

To celebrate this resounding success, a special high-performance Escort was created by Ford for sale to the general public – the Escort Mexico. The Escort Mexico was to be Ford's best-selling performance model (over 7,000 sold in four years) until the RS 2000 Mk 2 came along in 1976.

Just as in 1974, 1975 saw only two new cars from Scalextric, the BRM P160 and the Datsun 260Z.

The BRM had a remarkably long career for a Formula 1 car, making its début in the South African Grand Prix at Kyalami in 1971 and still being pressed into service for the 1974 season opener in Buenos Aires. The Scalextric P160 was modelled on the car raced by Swiss driver Jo Siffert and Brit Peter Gethin in 1971. Both drivers won Grands Prix that season, Siffert's victory coming at the Zeltweg circuit in Austria, where he secured pole position for BRM, the first time that had happened since Graham Hill at Watkins Glen in 1969.

Gethin's win was played out as if it were scripted by a Hollywood screenwriter. Three cars were dicing for the lead at the end of the Italian Grand Prix, each playing a cat-and-mouse game and looking for a 'tow' in the drag 'shadow' behind the car in front in order to then 'sling-shot' out in an overtaking move that would send them hurtling across the finish line. Gethin ultimately managed to outsprint Ronnie Peterson's March in the final straight and he took the chequered flag to triumph by just one hundredth of a second, setting an all-time record that day for winning a Grand Prix by the smallest margin ever.

Back in the rally world, the Datsun 260Z was Scalextric's rough-and-tumble car for 1975. Bigger sister to the 240Z, the 260Z had lost a little of the 240's sporting good looks, with a slightly stretched body, more room inside and a bigger engine. The 2.6-litre unit gave the heavier car a marginal top-speed advantage over the 2.4-litre 240Z, but by the time it was rallying on the international scene the competition was

such that it had little chance of emulating the success of the 240. Datsun's purpose in fielding 'the Z Cars' in rallies was, just like any other manufacturer, to promote sales, particularly back home in Japan and in the lucrative North American market. To that end, the company's preferred events were the Monte Carlo and the Safari rallies, both of which were well known and respected in Japan and the US.

Above Intended primarily for the US market, the 1975 Corvette and Mustang dragsters never appeared in a UK catalogue

Right The front cover of the 1976 catalogue featured Niki Lauda's Ferrari 312T

Although they never won the Monte, the 240Z did triumph in the Safari Rally on a couple of occasions and the rugged Z cars gave good accounts of themselves in countless other competitions including the RAC.

More Mighty Minis

The year 1976 was a time of contrasts, with more highs and lows than a yo-yo on a seesaw on a rollercoaster. In the sea between Britain and Iceland raged the 'Cod War', a term which conjures up fantastic images of battle-crazed armies of fish slugging it out on the seabed but which was actually a far more mundane dispute over fishing rights and territorial waters. If that was one of the lows, then the simultaneous first commercial flights of the British and French Concorde aircraft were surely one of the highs. In America, they celebrated 200 years of independence by deciding that they wouldn't let Concorde land at their airports as it was too noisy by far. Just as well it wasn't going there, then.

While America throbbed and pouted

Right The Ford Escort Mexico became Ford's best-selling performance car

Left The Mini 1275 GT appeared in Scalextric form in 1976

with patriotic fervour, Britain gobbed and pogoed as the Sex Pistols announced Anarchy in the UK. None of this caused too much of a distraction for James Hunt, who became Formula 1 World Champion driving for McLaren. 'Hunt the Shunt', as he became known (and that's the polite version), due to his propensity for letting his car get up close and personal with other cars during races, took the championship after he raced on through torrential rain during the Japanese Grand Prix when his nearest championship rival, Niki Lauda, retired due to the adverse conditions.

There are seldom any adverse conditions on the Scalextric track, and for 1976 there were three new Formula 1 cars. The Brabham BT44B was a development of the BT44 which first raced in 1974. It proved to be incredibly fast in a straight line, if a little temperamental, and scored its first Formula 1 victory at Kyalami in South Africa. Coincidentally,

Kyalami was the place where Brabham had last won a Formula 1 race four years previously. The Scalextric version of the car was resplendent in the Martini racing colours of the 1975 car which won in Brazil at the hands of Carlos Pace and in Germany with Carlos Reutemann driving.

The second Scalextric Formula 1 offering wasn't actually a new car but it did boast a whole new colour scheme. The Shadow was now available in the black paint scheme which, with a few exceptions, would be the livery in which most Shadow cars raced. The UOP logo of Shadow's main sponsor, United Oil Products, now adorned the car too.

The Tyrrell 007 was the third new car. The 006 was the car in which Jackie Stewart had won his third and final (he retired from racing) World

Championship in 1973, and the 007 was, naturally, Tyrrell's new car for 1974. Jody Scheckter and Patrick Depailler were Tyrrell's two new drivers and Scheckter soon proved himself by winning both the Swedish and British Grands Prix in 1974. He followed up in 1975 with a win on his home turf in

Clubman had been introduced in 1969 with a flat front that changed the look of the car, although it was still recognisably a Mini. The 1275 GT version was launched at the same time, using the bigger 1275 cc engine from the Mini Cooper as opposed to the standard Clubman 998 cc unit.

Below The 'Porsche 935 Turbo' became an enduring model for Scalextric. This is a 1980 car with extra gold decoration

South Africa. As with the real car, the Scalextric Elf Tyrrell 007 was in blue with white detailing, notably on the very prominent Elf oil company's (Tyrrell's sponsors) logo.

In the year that the four millionth Mini rolled off the British Leyland production line, Scalextric launched a new (to Scalextric) version. The Mini

The Clubman was every bit as successful in club and saloon car racing as the original Mini had been and, indeed, such was the affection for the old shape that it remained in production. In fact, Minis with the rounded front were held in such affection by the general public that they would stay in production for almost 20 years after the Clubman

Above The Tyrrell 007 brought Jody Scheckter a win on his home turf in South Africa

was discontinued in 1980. The existence of the 1275 GT, however, spelt the end (for the time being at least) of the Mini Cooper, whose production ceased in 1971. The famous 'Cooper' badge would reappear on the bonnets of Minis again towards the end of the little car's record-breaking production run.

The 1275 cc unit might have given more power than the smaller Mini engines, but it still wasn't enough for some prominent drivers like Peter Baldwin who, in 1975, dumped the British Leyland engine from his Mini and installed a Ford engine, gearbox and transmission. He raced the car in various Special Saloon competitions where most of the field would often comprise Minis in one form or another.

The year 1977 was Queen Elizabeth II's Silver Jubilee, when she celebrated 25 years on the throne. The Sex Pistols joined in by topping the UK singles charts with their version of 'God Save the Queen'. Meanwhile in America, screaming tartan armies of girls greeted The Bay City Rollers on their US tour and Elvis died.

Scalextric toasted the Queen's Jubilee with another Martini. This time the white, red and blue livery appeared on a Porsche Turbo 935. This car, in the classic Porsche shape established by the 911 in the mid-Sixties, would totally dominate its class of racing in a way that was becoming almost expected of any new Porsche. The 935 competed in Group 5 racing events and the factory cars were fielded for the World Championship of Makes. Turbocharged engines were what everyone was racing with in this class in 1976 and the 935's 4-litre engine produced around 590 bhp – that's ten times as much power output as the previously mentioned Mini 1275 GT. The 935 swept the board in the 1976 World Championship, despite stiff competition from BMW with its 3.5 CSLs, except for one race. At the Nürburgring, private entrant Reinhold Höst took the chequered flag at the wheel of a Porsche 908.

One of the 1976 team cars didn't fare so well at Silverstone, though. Rather than the clink of Martini glasses to celebrate the start of another race, Porsche's sponsors heard a rather alarming clunk as the clutch in Formula 1 driver Jackie Ickx's car fell apart on the starting line. It took the mechanics the best part of two hours to replace it, whereupon Ickx proved what a good job they had done by breaking the lap record to catch up with the rest of the racers. He finished an honourable second last.

Although it wasn't included in the World Championship of Makes, the 935 also flexed its muscles at Le Mans. It came in fourth in 1976 when a 936 actually won, and third in 1977, when a 936 also won. Porsche 935s then came in fifth, sixth, seventh and eighth in 1978 before taking first, second and third in 1979. One of the co-drivers of the second-placed car was none other than 54-year-old movie star Paul Newman.

Six-wheel Wonders

'Speed, action, excitement. That is what Scalextric is all about' claimed the catalogue for 1977, and the other two new cars with which you could create speed, action and excitement were the McLaren M23 and the JPS Lotus 77.

The McLaren M23 was the car in which James Hunt became World Champion in 1976, although by then it was rather long in the tooth. The car had first been fielded by McLaren in 1973, and it was the first car with which McLaren raced in their now-famous red and white Marlboro colours. The M23's long and illustrious racing career included victories in the Swedish and Canadian Grands Prix in 1973, four Grand Prix wins and the Constructors' Cup for McLaren in 1974, three wins in 1975, and six wins and the World Championship for Hunt in 1976. Naturally, many changes and improvements were made to the car during all that time, but

Below The March 240 bearing the original racing colours **(right)** with the Rothmans cigarette logo and in revised form **(left)** with cigarette advertising removed

Left The McLaren M23 displays its Marlboro cigarette sponsors brand on the cover of the 1977 catalogue

very few cars in Formula 1 can claim to have lasted so long.

In stark contrast, the Lotus 77 lasted only one season and won only one Grand Prix. To be fair, the 77 wasn't really built to last. It was something of a transitional car, taking the Lotus team from the 72 to the hugely successful Lotus 78 that would help to make Mario Andretti World Champion and bring the Constructors' Cup to Lotus in 1978. The one win for the 77 also came with Italian-American Andretti at the wheel. One of the world's greatest racing drivers, Andretti had won just about everything there was to win in motor sport in the US before turning to Formula 1 for a new challenge. His victory in the 77 came on the same rain-drenched Mount Fuji circuit in Japan where Lauda abandoned the race and Hunt came in third, scoring enough points to win the Championship.

By this time, Scalextric models were becoming ever more intricate, with great attention paid to accurate detail, and technical advances in the production process allowing for rising quality of manufacture. One of the great steps forward was a new printing process, tampo printing, which enabled Scalextric cars to have numbers, designs and sponsors' logos printed with superb clarity on the model, the process adhering, within reason, to the curves, bends and fine detail on the models' mouldings. Previously, decoration for the models had come in the form of transfers or stickers which you stuck on the car once you got it home from the shop. The trouble was that these transfers could become brittle after a while and start to flake off, succumbing to the heat produced by the motor after extensive non-stop, high-speed racing as well as extensive non-stop, high-speed impact with other cars, the floor, the furniture, the walls, and, if you took the High Hump Bridge too fast, the ceiling. Tampo printing would still look good after even the most horrendous multi-car or hardwood furnishings pile-ups.

The outlook at Scalextric moving into the late Seventies was still one of caution. The models the company was marketing were easily recognisable modern racing models and the number of new models introduced each season was generally quite modest.

The competition for that portion of hard-earned cash that the public set aside for leisure pursuits was growing ever more intense. Home computers and basic computer games to be played on your television were soaring in popularity. Microsoft sales broke through the $1 million ceiling like a Lotus 77 off the High Hump Bridge in 1978, and the Taito Corporation unveiled its new Space Invaders game. As if stealing the time and money of Scalextric's potential customers wasn't bad enough, the other essential ingredient for the enjoyment of mini model motor racing – imagination – was also under attack. Sci-fi fantasy blockbuster movies *Close Encounters* and *Star Wars* had both been released in 1977, with the most amazing special effects ever seen in the cinema, to be followed by *Superman* in 1978. 'You'll believe a man can fly' was how they advertised

Superman. How does a little plastic driver with no legs compete with that? And if all of that wasn't bad enough, you could even be banned from using your Scalextric set in the living room if Mum was concentrating on the new TV drama *Dallas*.

Nevertheless, there was cautious optimism at Scalextric, and three new models in the 1978 catalogue to whet the appetites of both living-room and club racers alike. Scalextric 'drivers' now had the opportunity to do what no Formula 1 driver had done and race the March Ford 240. Like the Tyrrell P34, the March 240 had six wheels. The concept was actually under consideration to varying degrees by a number of Formula 1 constructors. The theory was that the more rubber you could get in contact with the track, the better traction you would have and the faster you would go. You could also have smaller wheels which would cause less drag. In fact, the March 240's handling proved to be terrible, and the company did not have the financial resources to pour vast amounts of cash into developing the six-wheel car. The 240 never turned a wheel in anger.

The Tyrrell P34 did somewhat better, winning the 1976 Swedish Grand Prix with Jody Scheckter behind one of its many wheels and turning out good enough performances throughout the season to see Tyrrell lying third in the Constructors' Cup. The 1977 season produced more questions than answers for the six-wheeler, though, and the P34 suffered from much the same lack of development funds as the March 240. By 1978 no one really believed in the concept any more, and the idea of six-wheeled racing ground to a six-wheeled halt.

Another of the new models ·for 1978 was the TR7. Launched by British Leyland in 1975, the Triumph TR7 was the latest addition to Triumph's

TR series, although when it was first unveiled at the Geneva motor show most sports car enthusiasts were appalled. The TRs had always been very much the traditional British sports car, with traditional British sports car design and, oh yes, a soft top. This wedge-shaped monstrosity wasn't even a convertible! Leyland had fallen foul of a nasty rumour that the US government was about to ban convertibles on safety grounds. The TR7 was introduced without a convertible option, and it would be five years before the short-lived production run of the TR7 drophead.

Undeterred by the barrage of criticism, Leyland decided to take its ugly duckling rallying, equipped with the 16-valve engine and gearbox from Triumph's Dolomite Sprint sports saloon. The venture was not a huge success, with the car breaking down more often than a Hollywood starlet sporting a high-maintenance hair-do in a howling hurricane.

Following a long strike at the Leyland plant on Merseyside, where the TR7 was produced, the TR7 V8 finally saw the light of day in 1980. This was the car that had always been intended for America, and under the bonnet it had Rover's Buick-derived 3.5 litre V8. For the US market this car was designated the TR8 and convertible versions of both the TR7 and TR8 were now available. For Leyland's works rally team, the new power unit changed everything. They had V8 power a full two years before the production car was launched, and Rally ace Tony Pond won with the TR8 on its first outing in 1978 at the Ypres 24-hour race. He followed that up with another win in the Manx International Rally, although he didn't do so well in the Tour of Corsica when both of the Leyland cars' gearboxes seized up after what appeared to be a deliberate act of sabotage.

Left Unlike the March 240, the Tyrrell P34 did see some racing success, but the Spanish-built Scalextric car never appeared in a UK catalogue

Scandalous! That certainly wouldn't happen on the Scalextric track. Not much . . .

Sadly, the TR7 was just proving its worth when production ceased in 1981 and the Leyland team had no choice but to withdraw the TR from rallying.

The third new car from Scalextric for 1978 was the BMW Turbo 320. BMW had been slugging it out with Ford in the European Touring Car Championship since their epic 1973 battle when BMW fielded drivers such as Niki Lauda and Derek Bell against Ford's Capri drivers Jody Scheckter, Jackie Stewart and Emerson Fittipaldi. BMW's CSL 'Batmobile' saw serious action in a number of different guises, and the Scalextric version was based on the Group 5 3.2-litre turbocharged version as driven by Swede Ronnie Peterson. A potential 1000 bhp was available from the engine, although it

was usually only tuned to produce about 800 bhp, still making it the most powerful competitor ever built. It could hit 185 mph, but was not as reliable as lesser incarnations of the CSL.

The road versions of the car, some of which displayed a 'Batmobile' rear-wing kit and some of which didn't, were capable of up to around 145 mph – perfectly legal on the speed-limitless German autobahns, but more than enough to have the boys in blue in most other countries introduce you to one of their finest concrete accommodation suites for a lengthy spell . . . if they could catch you.

The Superhero Saloon

The Batmobile was so called because the rear wing made it look more as if it had been sketched by a comic book artist than drafted by an automotive

Right Patrick Depailler in the Tyrrell 007 on the cover of the 1978 catalogue

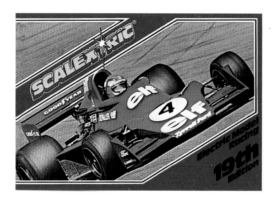

Below The Scalextric TR7 appeared in a number of different liveries and this model was designed with the pop-up headlights in the popped-up position

was fending off the shatteringly fast Leyland Jaguar XJ 5.3 coupés. Although they had plenty of 'get up and go', the big cats were found sadly lacking in the 'slow down and stop' department. Without the brakes to counter their speed, the Jaguars regularly left the BMWs to thunder home in the lead with swarms of Porsches buzzing in their wake. The seasoned CSLs won all eleven of the 1977 European Touring Car Championship events.

The Batmobile was also the scourge of the racing circuits for years in America, notably in the 1975/6 IMSA series for which a special-bodied car with even more bulges and buttresses was prepared by BMW. One of the most prolifically successful racing saloons of all time, the CSL appeared in a multitude of different colour schemes for a variety of different teams, including the vivid orange of BMW specialists Alpina.

Superhero saloons aside, the emphasis for Scalextric in 1979 was most definitely on Formula 1, with four new models to add to the Grand Prix collection.

engineer. It was back in Scalextric form in 1979 in a brand-new livery. The white body with red, blue and purple bands was the uniform of the BMW works team which had been showing the world how to handle endurance and touring car races since 1973. Ford's 3-litre Capris were the ones with the rear view of the CSL's famous wing in 1973, and in 1977 the CSL on which Scalextric's new model was based

The Elf-sponsored Tyrrell 008 looked remarkably conventional compared to its Tyrrell predecessor, the P34, especially when it came to the wheels. It had just one at each corner – a total of four compared to the P34's rather extravagant six. Conventional it may have been, but it made its mark at once when Patrick Depallier took third place in the Argentinian Grand Prix at Buenos Aires in January 1978. Depallier and his team mate, Didier Pironi, went on to finish in among the leaders in every Grand Prix that season bar the Swedish race, where both retired, and Monaco, where Depallier won.

Although impressive compared to the fairly dismal season they had endured with the P34 the previous year, the 008 hadn't performed well enough to persuade Tyrrell's sponsors to stay with the team. At the end of the season secondary sponsors City Bank and main sponsors Elf, whose logo had been emblazoned on Tyrrell cars since 1968, withdrew.

Part of the reason for Elf's change of heart was, perhaps, that they were backing another horse in the Grand Prix race. This came in the shape of the Elf

Renault Turbo RS-01, Scalextric's second new Formula 1 car for 1979. The RS-01 had been unveiled in 1977 and boasted an innovative 1500 cc turbocharged engine at a time when most Formula 1 teams were running with engines of twice that capacity. Elf might well have done better to stick with Tyrrell. The RS-01 proved hopelessly unreliable and by the end of the 1978 season the team had amassed the grand total of just three Grand Prix points. It would take a new car for 1979 before Renault's turbo engine started to show its promise, eventually persuading all of the major constructors to invest in turbo technology. In 1978, alas, the turbo was a turkey. Had this been *The Weakest Link*, Renault would have been shown the door.

The team holding the door open for them would doubtless have been Ferrari. Having won the Constructors' Cup in 1975, 76 and 77, come second in 1978 and reclaimed the title in 1979, Ferrari's joyful prancing horse had plenty to neigh about. The Scalextric Ferrari for 1979 was the 312 T3 as driven by Gilles Villeneuve and Carlos Reutemann. Good as it was, the Ferrari was no match in 1978 for the

Left The Batmobile in Alpina-style racing colours for 1980

Right Formation driving for the 1979
catalogue cover

all-conquering Lotus team, which won 8 of the 16 Grands Prix that season, relegating Ferrari to second place in the championship despite the T3's five wins.

Lotus's dominance in 1978 was due to their new ground-effect 'wing-car', a design that used the air flow over and around the bodywork of the car to help force it down onto the tarmac and give it greater traction. It was a dramatic new idea, subsequently adopted by Ferrari (and almost everyone else) for their 312 T4 in 1979. The only constructor brave enough to follow Lotus's example in 1978, though, was the new Wolf team. Austrian/Canadian businessman Walter Wolf had whetted his appetite for Formula 1 with the Williams team, eventually buying out founder Frank Williams in 1976. Williams would go on to reinvent the Williams team, of course, leaving Walter Wolf Racing to flex its muscles in 1977.

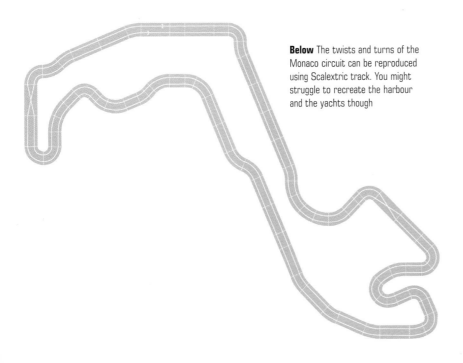

Below The twists and turns of the
Monaco circuit can be reproduced
using Scalextric track. You might
struggle to recreate the harbour
and the yachts though

The team won its first-ever Grand Prix in Buenos Aires and took two more wins that season. The introduction of the Wolf WR5 'wing-car' in 1978 was a bold move but the copycat failed to emulate the success of the Lotus, mechanical problems spoiling some promising race performances.

Scalextric's 1979 crop of four Grand Prix cars all certainly looked great on the plastic track, but why the emphasis on Formula 1 as opposed to the other forms of motor sport that had always been represented in 1:32 scale in the past? The various fuel crises and the escalating cost of going racing had had a detrimental effect on most forms of motor sport in the bleak mid-Seventies, but Formula 1 had survived relatively unscathed and consolidated its glamorous image through gradually increasing worldwide TV coverage. The cars themselves were also growing ever more sophisticated. Computers were now becoming commonplace but, despite the constantly evolving use of high technology in the design of Formula 1 cars as well as in their diagnostic and management systems, the Grand Prix arena was still the realm of racing heroes. Here was a ferociously powerful machine being thrown around a racetrack by a real live human being at speeds fast enough to leave the rest of us wondering if that third Weetabix at breakfast was really such a good idea. You might only be able to see his helmet bobbing around in the cockpit, but there was a living, breathing man in there piloting that car and risking his life. Driving a Formula 1 car was a dangerous game – there were real risks being taken and there was the real thrill of uncompromising competition on the track.

The risk factor might not have been quite as acute on the Scalextric track, but the growing interest in Formula 1 made perfect sense of Scalextric's Grand Prix programme. The competition thrills were all there in miniature, and the magic element of imagination was there too, tapping into the adrenalin reserves. That element of direct competition was something that couldn't really be matched by the monotonous burping of the Space Invaders arcade games that hit the UK in 1979, and even listening to the delicious Debbie Harry on your portable cassette-radio didn't add much of a thrill to trying to solve that pesky Rubik's Cube puzzle.

Scalextric still had plenty to offer in terms of sheer entertainment, and as the Seventies drew to a close the future of model motor racing was shining brighter than the glare from Ferrari's trophy cabinet.

Below The WR5 was an attempt by Walter Wolf Racing to copy the successful Lotus 'wing-car' formula

Steering Wheels and Horses on Sticks

By the end of the 1960s the list of Scalextric products was as long and unmanageable as a hippy's head of hair, and the financial problems which beset the company meant that the range required more than just a quick trim – drastic surgery was in order.

Maintaining availability of almost three dozen cars, a bewildering array of track sections and enough accessories to stock an entire hobby shop was no longer financially viable, especially with the investment required in the new You Steer system.

The 1970 catalogue featured special sets to 'convert' your existing track to You Steer. They consisted of either one Javelin car, an island hazard to steer around and a hand controller with steering wheel; or a Mirage and Ferrari P4 cars, two new hand controllers and two islands to steer around.

Steering-wheel-equipped hand controllers were available separately, along with a motor/steering unit to convert existing Javelin, Mirage, P4, Miura and Ford 3L models. Track borders of various kinds had been available since the early Sixties and borders were now seen as almost essential to stop your wildly skidding You Steer car slewing off the track. Island hazards and strangely medieval-looking archway hazards were also required to give you something to steer round. On top of all that, there were three new You Steer car and track complete sets on offer. There weren't too many takers.

To be fair, the regular Scalextric shop window was still tempting enough to keep most Scalextric fans' noses pressed firmly against it. Distracting little details like miniature tool boxes, oil cans and car jacks to scatter around your pit-stop still appeared in the catalogue, and there remained two dozen cars in the Scalextric stable.

Below Jump Jockey – perhaps a Galloping Hooves sound effects record might have helped . . . or maybe not

Funny we should mention stables, because it brings us in a barely contrived way to the last four pages of the 1970 catalogue, which were devoted to the Jump Jockey Electric Steeplechasing horse racing sets. There were extra accessories for the Jump Jockey sets, too. Disappointingly, there were no galloping hoofs or breathless commentators on a sound-effects record, but there was an amusing 'shying hazard', consisting of a group of spectators at a rail which provided 'Super excitement when horses shy unpredictably on this unique hazard – clockwork operated'. Incredible – a clockwork-operated stampede with spectators in danger of being trampled to death. There was also a Jump Rider on a trail bike, hurtling over fences like Steve McQueen jumping the barbed wire into Switzerland in *The Great Escape*, only hopefully with greater success. The biker and Mr McQueen take us neatly

and with great relief back to motor sport again.

The introduction of new accessories had slowed to crawling pace by 1972, but in among the straw bales, picket fences and track supports on offer that year was a pack of four special low-profile tyres on new wheels. Speeding into the pits and whipping off your wheels during a Scalextric race was never going to recreate the drama and tension of a real pit-stop. Jackie Stewart probably never had a pit-stop where one of his wheels rolled out of the bedroom door and bounced all the way down the stairs. Mind you, he probably never had a giant hand drop out of the sky and pluck his car off the track, either. No, the real value of the new wheels was in being able to replace the inferior tyres of older cars with new ones that would give better grip, helping you to stay on the track and keep racing.

Above The Jump Jockey horses galloped along with the aid of an electric trolley below the track, as did the Jump Rider biker

Right The You Steer hand control was difficult to use in a race situation unless you had at least three hands

No new elements of track had been forthcoming from Scalextric since the Sixties until the new 60° banked curve came along in 1973. Creating banking on the corners of your track layout had been possible before, of course, but it usually required careful coordination of the track sections and precarious arrangement of the banking supports to prevent any sagging where the sections joined. The new banked curve was entirely self-supporting, and tilted at an angle that would leave the more casual, 'windows open' driver scraping his elbow along the track. The old banking systems, although faster than a flat corner, still meant that you had to slow down significantly to take the bend without it looking like you were training for your pilot's licence, but the cars didn't fly off so easily on the new, steeper bank. In fact, it gave something of a slingshot effect onto the straight, where you could go for that elusive scale speed of 200 mph.

Unfortunately, the 60° bank proved too much for some cars, particularly the 1980 Ford Escort with

Below Slightly revised Javelin models were the first of the You Steer cars

working lights. Its front wheels fouled the arches when it hit the steep bank and the car's guide had to be built up to raise the wheels clear of the track. This was a shame, because it affected the overall handling of the car, although other Scalextric cars were designed to ride with the front wheels off the track in order to maintain the electrical contact more effectively.

The Perils of Spectating

Perhaps the lack of new components at this juncture prompted the highlighting of the decal stickers in the 1973 catalogue. The decals had been issued with new cars and sets since the Sixties and were largely superseded by the introduction of printed decoration in the mid-Seventies, although Scalextric did continue to supply decal sheets in the boxes along with new cars. For now, though, your only option in decorating your car was to soak your decals in a saucer of water, slide them off the backing sheet and position them carefully on the car, where they would dry out and adhere. Without doubt the decals made the models look more realistic. It was far more fun racing a car round the track decked out in STP Oil, Champion Sparkplugs, Dunlop or Ferodo logos than it was racing naked. The cars, that is, not you. On the other hand . . .

New for 1975 was a 50-Lap Counter with its own special track section. It notched up a lap every

Above Decals as supplied with and applied to a Ferrari P4. Those with a sense of humour might have wanted to use the Leyland badge to claim the Italian supercar for Britain

Right The 60° banked curve as it appeared in the 1973 catalogue looking for all the world like a normal curve stood on end

Right There's always room for another lap counter and 1975's version was manually operated by the cars themselves

Right The Auto Start in 1976 added to the atmosphere of the circuit and eliminated blatant cheating on the start line

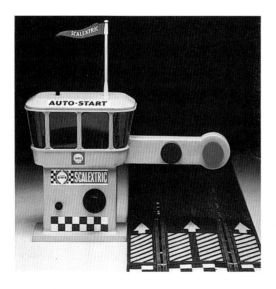

time a car crossed its short piece of track. This wasn't a new idea, a number of different lap counters having previously been produced, and it would have been sneered at by anyone who had the awesome electric 999 Lap Counter of 1969. Still, it did come with the new Speed Computer.

The Speed Computer was included in every new Scalextric set. Far from being a state-of-the-art electronics package, the Speed Computer was a simple cardboard disc affair. All you had to do was work out the overall length of your track (the lengths of different track sections were printed on the reverse of the Speed Computer) and time your car over one lap. Rotate the dials on the disc to align your time and distance and the pointer told

you your average speed. Rumours that it is still in use to calculate British railway timetables are totally unfounded.

New for 1976 was the Auto Start System. Up until now if two of you were racing, one of you always had to say 'GO!' This was frustrating in the extreme if you had a cousin who would jump the start by pretending he had a stammer. The Auto

Start put an end to such gamesmanship with a three-stage signal light system. Cunningly disguised as a race control tower, the Auto Start incorporated a boom which stretched out over the track bearing a red and a green light. It signalled continuous red for practice laps, flashing red to warn you to take your positions on the special starting grid, and green for go. The electrical power came from the track, but the lights were changed by a clockwork switch system, so no one was in charge of flicking the switch with a stammering finger.

New grandstand and pit-stop buildings came

along in 1978, accompanied by a selection of pit crew and spectator figures. The spectators were even worse off here than they were watching the Jump Jockey races. If they stood too close to the track when a You Steer car came sliding round the bend with its tail out they'd be eating carpet quicker than you could say Axminster. You had to paint the figures yourself and, while the grandstand and pit shelter looked the part, they were a far cry from the small hamlet's worth of buildings that had been available a few years before.

One of the final innovations of the 1970s was Penalty Cards. Early Scalextric catalogues had given marvellous direction on how to organise different kinds of races to get the most out of your Scalextric set and supplied a helpful framework of rules for the races. In 1979, the catalogue advised how to arrange handicap races, multiple car races and timed races. There was also a collection of penalty cards which were issued with every new Scalextric set. Selected blind by each contestant, they represented, for example, one- or two-lap penalties for such things as a puncture, steering failure or mechanical breakdown. This was a way of introducing an element of luck into Scalextric racing which might offset any skill differential between the contestants unless, sadly, you were a duff racer and unlucky enough to choose a tough penalty card.

The penalty cards were a simple, low-cost way to add to the fun of Scalextric. In the 1980s, novelties, gadgets and gizmos would become far more sophisticated.

Left In the late Seventies, Penalty Cards could turn you from a front runner into a back marker

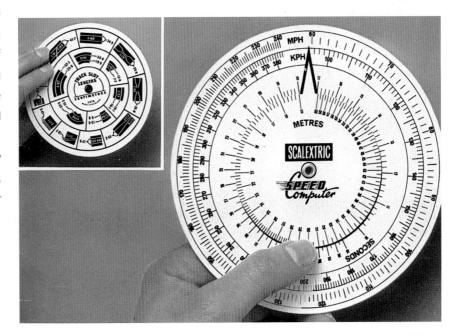

Below The Speed Computer was a simple device which did everything that later electronic versions would do, only in cardboard

Racing

into the

Computer

Age

Racing into the Computer Age

At the end of the Seventies it was time to boot up your hard drive and join the technological revolution. You finally had to admit that those long-haired nerds with the painfully uncool glasses were actually on to something with all their computer waffle. Clive Sinclair (later *Sir* Clive), who would surely have loved to have had long hair rather than a head that shone brighter than the fog-lamps on an Escort Mexico, launched his first ZX microcomputer and the home computer revolution was well and truly under way.

Having freed itself from the spangled grasp of glam rock, Britain was now locked in the firm grip of its first female prime minister, Margaret Thatcher, who had taken up residence in Downing Street in May 1979, and across the Atlantic former actor Ronald Reagan was about to take on his greatest starring role as president of the United States.

If the thought of all that proved too much for you, you could stick a Pretenders cassette in your new Sony Walkman and start planning another layout for your Scalextric track. The 1980 catalogue illustrated 21 different layouts for the six new sets on offer, with the top-of-the-range '600' set becoming the first Scalextric kit to retail at over £100 – £107.95 to be precise. It did, however, have four cars (Wolf, Brabham, Shadow and McLaren) with enough track to make a slightly skewed figure-of-eight four-lane circuit, and the component parts included in the set represented a saving of almost £30 over buying equivalent equipment individually.

Two brand-new cars were available from 1980 in the shape of the Ford Capri for Touring Car fans and the Ligier JS11 for Formula 1 fiends. Ford's *new* Capri (the name had been used on both a 1952 Lincoln and the 1961 Ford Consul coupé) was launched in February 1969, inspired

by Ford's immensely successful Mustang. Less inspiring was Europe's answer to the 'Pony Car', with its 1300 cc engine, which would have left it nuzzling the grass in the first furlong had it ever gone under starters' orders with the US thoroughbred. Nine months later a 3-litre V6 engine helped to pep up its performance, giving the standard production model a top speed of almost 115 mph with a 0–60 mph time of around 9 seconds. Advertised by Ford as 'The Car You've Always Promised Yourself', the Capri was intended as a family-friendly sports coupé with room in the back for a couple of kids providing that they didn't grow too big.

In competition the Capri scored its first success just three days after the car was launched. Mud and gravel expert Roger Clark drove a 3-litre, four-wheel-drive Capri to victory at the Croft Rallycross circuit in the north of England in front of millions of

ITV *World of Sport* viewers. Apart from the special competition cars, which also competed in the 1970–71 rallycross events in Britain, the Capri was never available with four-wheel-drive. Without the added traction of 4x4, however, the Capri would certainly have been left floundering in the mire as cheeky little Minis zipped past.

Rallycross attracted the biggest UK TV audiences and, therefore, the best publicity opportunities, but in Germany (the Capri was produced by Ford in both Halewood, England and Cologne, Germany) it was track racing that received most attention. The one to win was the European Touring Car Championship. By the start of the 1971 season Cologne's competition department had developed a car they reckoned was a winner – the Capri RS2600. A series of spectacular wins, including a 1-2-3 in Austria, proved them right, and works driver Dieter Glemser became European

Touring Car Champion, although Alfa Romeo pipped Ford at the post for the manufacturers' trophy. The following year, the works team completely dominated the ETC, winning all but one of the races. Meanwhile, in Finland, Timo Makinen added to the Capri's fast-growing list of racing honours by slip-sliding one round the world's coldest race circuits to become Finnish ice-racing champion.

The year 1973 saw the Capri's epic ETC battles with BMW's famous Batmobile, the Capri ultimately losing out to the massive power and clever

Left Capri Mark 1 with heavily modified bodywork in action on the track

Left Scalextric's Capri was based on the Mark III with a rear wing based on the Brooklyn Bridge

Left Capri and Datsun 260Z in action on the Flying Leap

Right Speedmaster flexed his muscles on the 1981 catalogue cover

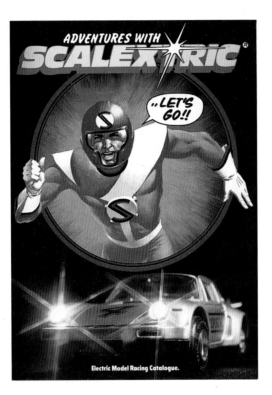

aerodynamics of the BMWs. Ford officially withdrew the Capri from motor sport at the end of 1974, but it raced on in the hands of privateers for a number of years. Gordon Spice reigned supreme as Group 1 British Saloon Car Champion in a variety of Capris from 1975 to 1980. The Scalextric 3-litre Capri is based on the Mark III body style that was introduced in 1978 and continued through to the end of Capri production in 1986. By that time, Ford had produced 1.92 million Capris and any child who had been crammed into the rear seat of a Mark I was now old enough to be sitting in the driving seat, giving Mum and Dad a turn in the back.

French sportsman (he played international rugby for France), businessman, car importer and construction boss Guy Ligier entered Formula 1 in 1976 and had won just one Grand Prix up to the appearance of the Ligier JS11 for the 1979 season. Drivers Jacques Lafitte, Patrick Depailler and Jacky Ickx, who took over from Depailler when Depailler was hospitalised after a hang-gliding accident, scored three fine wins and took Ligier to third place

Above How on earth did Speedmaster fit all those muscles into the tiny cockpit of the Williams FW07B?

in the Constructors' Championship. The Scalextric Ligier JS11 carried a Ligier logo rather than the logo of the team's sponsor, Gitanes cigarettes. It had been felt inappropriate for some time for tobacco companies' logos to appear on Scalextric models and Lotus (John Player Special and Camel), March (Rothmans), McLaren (Marlboro), Ferrari (Marlboro), Benetton (Mild Seven), Williams (Winfield) and Jordan (Benson & Hedges), among others, would all have their liveries subtly changed to exclude cigarette manufacturers' brand names from the Scalextric cars. Despite the ever-increasing number of enthusiasts' racing clubs, Scalextric was, after all, still a toy intended primarily for youngsters.

Tobacco advertising aside, a number of old Scalextric cars were spruced up with new paint jobs for 1980, including the TR7, BMW CSL, Porsche 935, Ford Escort, Mini Clubman, Brabham and Shadow. The only other new development apart from the Ligier and Capri was the return of the motorcycle and sidecar combination. A more modern design than the previous versions, which had been out of production for ten years, the new combos were light, powerful and just as hard to keep under control as the earlier models. Some might argue that racing these models needed greater skill, and therefore provided a greater challenge. Others just liked to imagine the horrified plastic expressions behind those full-face helmets as you sent them hurtling towards the Flying Leap. Fun for all, then.

Speedmaster, Stox & Cop Cars

Action and adventure were the name of the game in 1981 when Scalextric produced their 'Superhero Issue' catalogue. The catalogue was based around Scalextric's specially created,

illustrated comic book adventures of Speedmaster, 'the top test driver for one of the world's largest technological development companies'. During the course of his desperate battle against his evil rival Zadoc-Bar, Speedmaster had to rescue the boss's daughter utilising along the way almost every piece of Scalextric equipment presented in the catalogue. Sadly, he was never to drive the most appropriate Scalextric car for a superhero of his status – BMW's Batmobile.

The first car to feature in Speedmaster's 'Race of Death' adventure was 'an experimentally modified' Saudia Leyland Williams. Scalextric's version of the Formula 1 car was based on the 3-litre Cosworth V8-powered Williams FW07B, the car in which Alan Jones had taken five Grand Prix wins in 1980 to become World Champion. Jones's teammate, Carlos Reutemann, notched up one win and between them they secured the Constructors' Cup for Williams. Not bad for a team that had had to start virtually from scratch just three years before. They could hardly have done any better even with Speedmaster driving for them, although he would have struggled to fit his overstuffed, mighty-muscled, Spandex-sheathed frame into the cramped confines of a real F1 cockpit.

Speedmaster hurtled out of the top-secret research facility in the Saudia Leyland Williams in hot pursuit of a Porsche (new silver and gold versions of the Porsche were available) in which his boss's daughter had been kidnapped. Keeping up with the Porsche involved overtaking a Rover SD1 police car. This was a hot new model from Scalextric. Forget the glitzy real headlights of the Porsche and Escort Mexico, the Police Rover had real 'Blues 'n' twos' – a flashing roof-light and police-style siren. This was the ultimate in realism.

Right A matching set of Porsches was offered in 1982 in gold and silver

Right Both cars had working headlights and were available individually or in the Le Mans 24-hour set

Now you could go for the 200 mph scale speed with a traffic cop on your tail!

The big Rover was also available from Scalextric as a saloon racer. Most people might have thought of the Rover more as the sort of car your doctor would turn up in if you had a touch of the lurgy (this was 1981, remember, when you might have been lucky enough still to have a doctor who made house calls), but the SD1 had a more dashing side to its character, too, as a racing saloon. The 3.5-litre V8 SD1 was unveiled by Rover in 1976 and was immediately put to work on the track by racers who knew the versatility and reliability of the engine. The most successful racing version, the Vitesse, didn't arrive until 1982 and proceeded to make something of an exhibition of itself, regularly chalking up impressive performances at touring car events all over Europe. In 1983, the top three drivers in the British Touring Car Championship were all piloting the Rover Vitesse, although Andy Rouse in an Alfa Romeo took the title when the big Rovers were excluded due to new FIA regulations. The following year, the Rover Vitesse did take the title, driven by none other than the aforementioned Mr Rouse.

Back with Speedmaster and the Race of Death, our hero waves a cheery greeting to the traffic cops as he roars past, then manages to get himself captured by the enemy, conveniently enjoying a flashback to his Speedmaster recruitment selection when Zadoc-Bar was his biggest rival for the job. They raced against each other in motorcycle and sidecar combinations, Speedmaster suffering a sabotage Blowout while Zadoc-Bar came to grief on the Hump Back Bridge. Their next skill test was in endurance racing, with a Porsche 935 up against the new Westwood Racing liveried Ford Escort (Scalextric were based in Westwood in Margate).

Speedmaster survived more skulduggery before going on to face Zadoc-Bar in a Super Stox race.

The 'Fenderbender' and 'Stickshifter' stock cars were a complete innovation from Scalextric. Available individually and in a special Super Stox set, these cars could swivel on their guide blades, spin through 180° and set off in the opposite direction, the first time you had ever been able to do this on a Scalextric track . . . deliberately. They also had detachable body panels which they would shed in spectacular fashion when they were crashed or rammed, the first time you had ever been able to smash a car to

Above The original Police Rover had flashing blue lights and a siren. This later model, seen cutting up a Pontiac Firebird, had no siren. Pinching your little sister provided a substitute noise

Below The Super Stox cars were the first Scalextric models actually designed to fall apart

Above In 1982 the Brabham BT49 appeared in Scalextric form

models. The Brabham BT49 was the only Formula 1 car, but it had certainly earned its place on the Scalextric track.

In 1980, Brazilian Nelson Piquet, in only his second full season in Formula 1 and with Brabham, completed his season by coming second in the World Championship driving the BT49. He equalled his 1980 total of three Grand Prix wins in 1981, this time winning the World Championship outright. It was the first time Brabham had produced a World Champion driver since Denny Hulme in 1967 and before that Jack Brabham himself in 66.

In complete contrast to the 3-litre V8 Ford Cosworth-engined Brabham came Scalextric's other track car for 1982, the 1.3-litre Leyland Metro. Intended as a replacement for the Mini (which would actually go on to outlive the Metro), the Metro was an unloved town car designed for your granny to be able to park with ease when

bits on a Scalextric track . . . deliberately. Or maybe not. The idea was to bring some of the excitement of banger racing to the small-scale track, and with a chicane and crossroads in the set to encourage as much contact as possible, the attrition rate was something akin to letting an infinite number of babbling maniacs drive as fast as they could with no regard whatsoever for the rules of the road. Rather like driving in Italy, in fact.

Meanwhile, the Speedmaster's final run-in with Zadoc-Bar involves him racing his Saudia Leyland Williams against the Evil One's robot drivers. The tinheads are driving March, Brabham and Tyrrell cars. If Speedmaster loses, he will be vaporised by a bank of deadly laser cannons as soon as he crosses the finishing line. Just another day at the office. Naturally, Speedmaster outwits the bad guys, rescues the girl and blows Zadoc-Bar to smithereens in the process.

Speedmaster had either retired or pumped up his muscles so hard that he exploded by the time the next catalogue came along, and 1982 just wasn't the same without him. As a consolation Scalextric offered a clutch of irresistible new

she popped out to the shops. But then, so was the Mini, and if the Mini was good enough to go racing, then the new 'Mini Metro' surely had to be just as good. To be fair, the little cars put up spirited performances in their class in the British Saloon Car Championship and won outright every race in the Unipart Metro Challenge – but then every car in the Unipart Metro Challenge was a Metro, so they would, wouldn't they? It was a one-make race series.

Two Metros were available for 1982, one small package in Datapost livery as raced in the British Saloon Car Championship and one small fry in McCain Oven Chips livery as raced in the Metro Challenge. Both Scalextric models featured an incredibly cute working rear hatchback, so you could raise the tailgate to store traffic cones or tyres or pick up some shopping on the way home from the races.

Low-loading Roadtrains & Spinning Minis

If the Metro was one of British Leyland's smallest production vehicles, then one of the biggest must surely have been the T45 Roadtrain. Along with its flatbed 'Low Loader' sister, the Roadtrain offered a whole new Scalextric experience. This wasn't the vehicle you raced on the track, this was the vehicle that brought your racing car *to* the track, yet here it was presented as a track model in its own right. Driving this articulated Leyland truck was a completely different experience to that of racing a Saudia Leyland Williams or a Leyland Metro. Just like a real truck, the Scalextric Roadtrain was too big to go under most flyover bridges, and there were certain corners and other track features it just couldn't negotiate. On the other hand, you could detach the tractor section from the trailer and race it on its own. It incorporated a special weight in the

Above The spinning Mini. 'Now which way were we racing again?'

Right German sausage sandwich on the 1982 cover. Porsche and BMW flanked by two Metros, two Rovers, a TR7 and an Escort

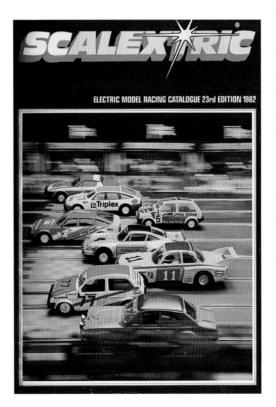

fuel tank to try to stop it from tipping over and it could make mincemeat of one of those piddling little Super Stox cars.

That provided another drawback, of course, in that the Roadtrain cab was superbly detailed, with chromed air horns, aerials, ladders and front crash grille, all of which could snap off at the mere

mention of the words 'Crossover Track'. It was possible to build a layout on which to race the monster Leyland trucks with their trailers but, like its humble cousin the Metro, there were more raceworthy versions waiting in the wings.

Also new for 82 were the Mini Banger Racers. The Mad Hatter Mini and Mini Ha-Ha were available, like the Super Stox cars, both individually and in a Banger Racing set. Also like the Super Stox, they could spin on their rotating guides through 180° or even 360°. They didn't spin without provocation, of course. On the whole, banked curves counteracted the tendency to spin on corners, but flat corners and chicanes sending the little devils all over the road. This might not have suited serious racers, but as far as all-out fun was concerned, Scalextric hadn't seen anything like the Banger Racers and Super Stox since 007 last sent his passenger on a one-way sunroof excursion.

Such innovations were indicative of the fact that Scalextric was starting to recover from the setbacks and market erosion it had suffered at the start of the Eighties. Although many of the 'new' models were really only re-liveried incarnations of previous cars, there were plenty of new ideas to keep Scalextric fans racing on into the night, not least the Ford Capri illuminated not only with bright white headlights but also with glowing red tail lights. If even that was too frivolous for the more serious-minded Scalextric racer, then the Bentley and Alfa Romeo models first seen in 1962 and out of production for around 15 years were back in 1982. With all of the superb detailing of the original models, these two were a delight for vintage car enthusiasts but fell foul of some of the new tightly curved track sections and the infamous 60° banking.

In 1983 came a continued drive to expand

the range, with a whole convoy of new vehicles queuing for shelf space in the toy shop. Some of these, again, were reworked versions of the old models, such as the TR7 with its pop-up headlights in the popped-up position. As any owner of an early TR7 will tell you, due to the somewhat uncertain nature of the electrics controlling the headlights, the popped-up position was often the only option. The TR7 also facilitated the return of the superhero, not Speedmaster in this case but Spiderman. Two TR7s with Spiderman illustrations on the bonnet and web designs on the roof were included in a special set marketed to capitalise on the popularity of the comic book and TV cartoon crime buster. Not one for arachnophobes.

The Spiderman TR7 set missed the 1983 catalogue, not appearing until the subsequent edition, but the MG Metro set made it onto the

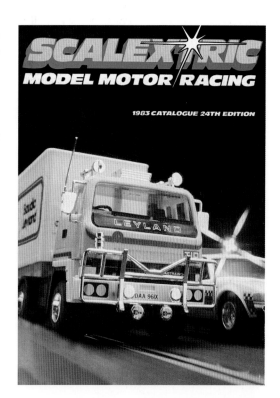

Left Tailgating trucker gets his just desserts on the 1983 catalogue cover

Left The Bentley and Alfa Romeo drivers are back and still giving each other the evil eye in 1982

Right The Spiderman TR7s were
shown in the 1984 catalogue on a
light-coloured track

back page. Having inherited the MG name and the use of the famous octagon logo during the various amalgamations that had transformed the British motor industry over the years, British Leyland decided to use MG's sporting heritage to its advantage by giving the humble Metro an MG badge. 'Badge engineering' wasn't a new thing, of course, the practice having become commonplace in the motor industry, and the Metro gained more than just a badge. The featherweight racer now packed a heavyweight punch, with a turbocharged engine that could catapult it up to over 130 mph. The Scalextric version still had the cute tailgate to accommodate the supermarket shopping run, though.

Above Hot Hatches – Ford Escort XR3 and MG Metro Turbo

A New Breed of Boy Racer is Born

The tailgate had become the defining feature of an 80s saloon car. The Rover SD1 had one, the Metro had one and the new Ford Escort XR3 had one, too. This was the era of the 'Hot Hatch', the souped-up saloons ultimately overpowering traditional sports cars like the MG Midget or Triumph Spitfire because they offered superior performance along with the refinement and convenience of a family car. Ford's Mark III Escort hit the showrooms amid much furrowing of brows among motoring enthusiasts. Surely this couldn't really be an Escort? It had one of those newfangled hatchback things and, good heavens, front-wheel drive! The new Escort, however, soon confounded its critics with the sporty XR3 model that could top 110 mph in standard form and whose sure-footed handling made it an ideal track racer or rally car. Just as they had done with the Capri, the Europeans lost no time in getting the new car on the racing circuit, and one of the Scalextric Escorts was based on the Autoveri

Left Like its real-life counterpart, the XR3 evolved into the XR3i and became a huge success

Right MG Maestro was a spectacularly ordinary car and the Scalextric version did little to change that

Motorsport racer which had started to make a name for itself in Germany in 1982.

The Escort XR3 was the only totally new car that made it into the 1983 catalogue, but among the latecomers that year was Leyland's MG Maestro, bigger brother to the Metro. Yet another family hatchback saloon pitched somewhere in between the Metro and the SD1, the 2-litre MG-badged version had an impressive turn of speed, although no amount of engine and suspension tweaking could disguise the fact that it was really an outstandingly ordinary family car. The Scalextric version even came equipped with a sun roof but, alas, no ejector seat.

Two other track stars which had missed the catalogue in 1983 but still appeared later in the year were the fabulous UFO and Old Glory racing trucks. Truck racing was fantastically popular in the United States and continental Europe and catching on fast in the UK. With around 1,200 horsepower on tap (more than twelve times the power output of a standard XR3) these mighty beasts thundered round the racetrack at phenomenal speeds. FIA, the authority which controlled European motor sports,

eventually decreed that the top speed of the turbocharged racing trucks should be limited to 100 mph for safety reasons, but the fastest trucks could still get there in around 10 seconds – faster than many contemporary sports cars.

The Scalextric racing trucks were recognisably based on the Roadtrain tractor unit, although they had a six-wheel chassis for extra stability and wore aerodynamic wings that made the Batmobile look positively underdressed. Passing through tunnels or under bridges on the slotted track was still a problem, but the sight of the monster trucks on the move was hugely evocative of the dust-and-thunder excitement of the real thing.

In contrast to those cars that didn't make it into the 1983 catalogue, the 1984 edition included one car that didn't make it into the shops. Ford's Sierra XR4i was big brother to the Escort XR3 in the same way that the Maestro was to the Metro. The 130 mph super saloon with its distinctive biplane rear wing was powered by the fuel-injected 2.8-litre V6 from the final version of the Capri and could top 130 mph. Unfortunately, although prototype models were featured in the catalogue,

the Scalextric XR4i never went into production.

There were plenty of other new arrivals to keep the fans happy, though, with the XR3 represented as the XR3i, Ford having added fuel injection to its hot hatch, and a number of other cosmetically enhanced models released, including the Rover SD1 in Track Marshal's livery with flags on the roof.

The Grand Prix range was 'expanded', with the Williams FW07B repainted in Formula 2 guise as the Casio-sponsored car driven by Jonathan Palmer and also as the *Grand Prix International* magazine-sponsored Formula 3 racer.

The real new cars for 1984 came in the shape of the Datsun King Cab 4x4 off-roaders, the incredible BMW M1 and the fantastic Audi Quattro.

The King Cab models were nicely detailed versions of the kind of pick-up trucks which are not only universally popular in America as everyday transport but are also raced both on and off the track. Racing off the track is a little complicated with Scalextric. It's unlikely that even the King Cab could cope with a slotless tabletop, and it would be totally at sea in the middle of a shag pile, so the King Cabs had a few tricks up their sleeves to

Left 1984's catalogue cover showed a typical scene during heavy traffic in Milan

Below These 1983 racing six-wheelers could show the old Formula 1 March and Tyrrell a thing or two

simulate the thrills and spills of off-road driving. The cars which came in the Track Busters set had a flip-over mechanism similar to that of the Mercedes in the old James Bond set. Race up behind one and nudge its bumper and a springloaded arm dropped down to send the truck tumbling off the track. The chromed roll-over bar was certainly put to good use. Sneaking up behind another car on a two-lane circuit isn't that easy, though, so a new feature was incorporated in the set – a controllable lane-switch system.

The idea was to race round to the lane-switch track section and the first one to hit his control button shifted his opposite number's car onto his lane. Naturally, you wanted your rival in front of you so that you could get in behind him and give him a good shunt. This wasn't for the serious racer, of course. In fact, the purists must have been growing increasingly horrified at the antics you could now get up to on the track. Minis that could turn round and race the wrong way? Stock-cars that smashed each other to bits? Trucks that rammed each other off the track? Surely the skill came in racing round the circuit, keeping your car in one piece and staying on the track? They may have had a point, but they probably never had much fun.

If the more traditional Scalextric cars modelled on high-powered racing machines were what the more serious-minded enthusiasts wanted, though, they couldn't go far wrong with the BMW M1 and the Audi Quattro.

The sensational BMW M1 represented an attempt by BMW to take on Porsche in the World Sports Car Championship, but the car was never fully developed and BMW eventually decided instead to go into Formula 1, supplying the engine for the Brabham BT 50. The plastic-bodied M1 with its 24-valve 6-cylinder engine did go racing, however, most spectacularly in 1979 and 1980, when they competed in specially staged single-make races in conjunction with the Formula 1 circus. Watching an entire field of the sleek machines competing on the track driven by Formula 1 aces such as Regazzoni, Pironi, Piquet and Lauda was a thrilling experience for racegoers. For most people, spectating at a racing circuit was as close as they would ever get to one of these supercars, as only 450 were ever made. The roadgoing M1, although less powerful than the racing version, still had a 277 horsepower engine that could take it from rest to 60 mph in just 5.5 seconds, so even if you did spot an M1 on the open road, you were unlikely to be able to keep it in sight for long.

Your best chance of getting close to an M1 was on the European rally circuit. The M1 first appeared in rally guise at the same time as the Lancia 037, in 1982, but it was by no means as competitive a car as the Lancia – too big, too wide and, even with its aluminium and glass fibre body panels, too heavy

for rallying. Spectators brave enough to stand their ground on the roadside grass verges of the Tour of Corsica in 1982 or the Antibes Rally in 1984 got the best view of the car in action. For the rest of us, the Scalextric version would just have to do.

The M1 may not have had much luck in rallying, and neither did the Audi Quattro. The difference was that the Audi didn't need luck. Announced at the Geneva motor show in 1980, the Quattro first showed its potential as a rally car in 1981, when Hannu Mikkola took the car through the special stages of the Algarve Rally in a special demonstration before the regular competition cars made their runs. Mikkola's times were recorded and, had he actually been competing in the Quattro, he would have won the rally by as much as 26 minutes.

The car's official début came the following year in the Monte Carlo Rally. Mikola was leading by almost six minutes after just six events but breakages, breakdowns and a closer view of the roadside scenery than he would have liked meant

Left The Scalextric Quattro had four-wheel drive just like the real thing

113

Right A modified Scalextric Quattro as raced by the enthusiast Chris Gregory

he eventually finished in a disappointing 91st place. The car had thrown down the gauntlet to the other manufacturers, though, its 2.2-litre turbocharged engine and four-wheel-drive system setting the benchmark for rally cars for years to come. There were three outright wins in 1981 in the Swedish, San Remo and RAC Rallies. The following year the Quattro came second in Monte Carlo but won the Swedish, Portuguese, San Remo, Acropolis, Brazilian, 1000 Lakes and RAC Rallies. Audi were the 1982 World Champions.

Although the engine would evolve as racing regulations changed, the results become monotonously repetitive, with first, second and third placings making Hannu Mikkola World Champion in 1983, Audi the World Champion manufacturers and Stig Blomqvist World Champion

driver in 1984. The Audi would continue to be competitive in international rallies for years to come, its sporting reputation galvanising sales of the Quattro road car, which also had four-wheel drive. The Scalextric Quattro had four-wheel drive as well, but while the distinguished engineers at Volkswagen/Audi had spent years and vast fortunes working out how to achieve the optimum weight and power distribution for maximum tractability from their four-wheel-drive system, the Scalextric boffins in Spain (like the M1 the Quattro was a Spanish-built car) simply linked the front and rear axles with a rubber band. If only the Germans had thought of that they could have saved themselves enough Deutschmarks for a lifetime's supply of lederhosen.

Hot Hatches and Red Braces

By 1985 the yuppie had arrived, probably in a VW Golf GTi (the hot hatch that was the epitome of cool) and Sir Clive Sinclair had blown his genius status by inventing the Sinclair C5, a plastic-bodied electric tricycle that provided the answer to the problem of commuting – get yourself a GTi.

If hot hatches were the cars to have, then Scalextric's 1985 catalogue had one of the hottest of the lot – the MG Metro 6R4. This wasn't the kind of Metro your granny could take to the shops. In fact, there wasn't any room for shopping. That cute tailgate now lifted up to reveal a 3-litre V6 engine. This Metro was a Group B rally car. Group B came about in 1982, when it was decided to throw caution to the wind and let manufacturers enter international rally events with cars that bore hardly

any relation to their roadgoing counterparts. It all seemed like a fun idea, but the manufacturers took the competitive element to the limit. Formula 1 designers were used to rework the basic cars and the Metro was given the full treatment by the Williams design team. It still looked a bit like a Metro, but it had been given a completely new chassis, a massive new engine where the fish fingers and chocolate chip cookies used to go, and it now had four-wheel drive.

The unrestricted delights of the Group B cars came to an end when the authorities finally decided to end the madness in 1986 and impose regulations on the building of rally cars in order to improve the safety of the events. Unfortunately, the Metro 6R4 came along too late for the inevitable teething troubles inherent in the creation of a car like this to be resolved, and the best result it achieved on the international scene was third place in the 1985 RAC Rally. There were wins in lesser events such as the Circuit of Ireland, Manx Rally and Antibes Rally in 1986, and the car won the French National Championship driven by Didier Auriol, also in 1986.

The Scalextric 6R4 appeared in the livery of the 'Ternco' team, the outfit around which the 1985 TV series *The Winning Streak* was based. It lacked the Batmobile-style roof-mounted rear wing of the real car, but the bulging wheel arches and front spoiler were a fair representation of the 6R4.

The MG Metro 6R4 was the only new model (and it was just a reworking of the previous Metro) to appear in the rather strange 1985 catalogue, which consisted of only eight new pages wrapped around a 1984 catalogue. Such cost-cutting measures were under way at Scalextric because, despite having had cause for optimism, the

Left Audi spent millions developing their four-wheel-drive system. Scalextric did it with a rubber band

company was once again facing a financial crisis. The XR4i model had been a victim of a rationalisation programme and, even more sadly, a number of redundancies had to be made among the factory workforce. There were happier times ahead, but for now the atmosphere in Margate was a sombre one.

The Road to Recovery

As Halley's comet sailed through the sky and Madonna begged her Papa not to preach, Scalextric took its first tentative steps towards recovery in 1986. Nine different sets appeared in the catalogue, along with a stable of some two dozen models many of which were labelled as new but most of which were really updates of older ones. The Datsun 260Z was pressed into service again in the racing colours of Bison Computers, with a recommendation that it be pitted against the faithful old Capri, which also received a new colour

Right The Metro 6R4 appeared in a variety of liveries

scheme. The XR3i was given an antipodean flavour in the shape of two models based on cars that had raced in Australia's Bathurst 24-hour race.

A variety of Metros were on offer in the catalogue, including one modelled on the Computervision 6R4 with which Tony Pond had done so well in the 1985 RAC Rally. It still lacked the aerodynamic aids which adorned the ultimate racing 6R4 but the catalogue described it as 'based on the prototype Metro 6R4'. And why not? Hadn't the finless D-type Jaguar in 1961 been based on a prototype too? You can't argue with a precedent.

The Quattro, M1, Porsches and Rover cop car were in there too, along with the scary trucks and two new versions of Datsun's kamikaze pick-up truck. The old Ferrari 312 T3 and Renault Turbo RS01 were recommissioned as Formula 2 cars in Tyler Autos and Graves Engineering racing livery, while woefully executed renditions of the Ferrari 312 T appeared as Track Burner and Track Ace cars.

In all fairness, the Track Burner and Track Ace cars, which were joined by a Track Flash version of a McLaren, were designed to be simplified models 'a little less elaborately finished' for younger racers and, more importantly, just half the price of Scalextric's regular Formula 1 cars. Similarly simplified Brabhams were offered, racing in Quodos and Kotzting Lager colours for a basic figure-of-eight Grand Prix set.

If all of that sounds like a load of old tat being tarted up to hide the fact that Scalextric had less new product to offer than it cared to admit, then you are listening with very cynical ears and you have yet to be introduced to the star of Scalextric's 1986 show, the Lancia Rally. Usually referred to by its type number, 037, the Lancia was a lovely two-door coupé based roughly on the Lancia Beta

Monte Carlo but with revised bodywork and a supercharged 305-horsepower engine that turned it into a worldbeater in international rally events.

Winners of the Acropolis, San Remo, New Zealand and Monte Carlo Rallies, to name but a few, the little white Lancias with the blue and red racing stripes of their Martini sponsors brought the Manufacturers' World Championship Trophy home to Lancia in 1983 and made World Champions out of Massimo Biasion in 1983, Carlo Capone in 1984 and Dario Cerrato in 1985. Like all the other cars the 037 struggled against the four-wheel drive of the Quattro, and the car that would take over its Lancia Martini racing colours, the Delta S4, was inevitably a 4x4.

Of the two Scalextric 037s for 1986, one naturally wore the Lancia Martini paintwork while the other was decked out in car audio producers Pioneer's logo. Both cars, like the Audi Quattro, originated in Spain.

The year 1987 was a golden one for sporting

Left The 1985 catalogue. Some trucks never learn

Left A rally action special for the 1986 catalogue cover

Left The Scalextric Lancia 037 in Martini racing colours but with the word 'Martini' replaced by the word 'Lancia'. The booze business suffered the same fate as the tobacco barons

heroes of the Americas, with the world's youngest-ever heavyweight boxing champion, Mike Tyson, adding the WBA title to his WBC belt and yachtsman Dennis Connor captaining the *Stars and Stripes* to victory, reclaiming the Americas Cup for the US. The Australians had audaciously wrested the cup from their clutches four years before, the first time since 1870 that the US had lost the trophy. Representing South America, Brazilian Nelson Piquet won his third Formula 1 World Championship title.

Scalextric's Formula 1 range benefited from the addition of two new cars in 1987. The Lotus Renault 98T was the car in which Ayrton Senna had led the World Championship for at least part of the 1986 season. In Detroit Senna fought his way back from seventh place after a puncture to take the lead and notch up an admirable win with a breathtaking display of pyrotechnics thrown in for good measure.

The showers of sparks were caused by his car bottoming out on the tarmac, it rode so low. In fact, Senna could control the ride height of the car using a device in his cockpit. His second and only other win of the season came hand in hand with more tyre trouble, not a puncture this time but a shortage of rubber. Senna stretched the endurance of his tyres to the limit in Spain to avoid having to stop, as Nigel Mansell was breathing down his neck in the

Left The Pontiac Firebird never looked quite right in Scalextric form

Williams Honda. In a nailbiting finish, Senna's increasingly unstable Lotus held off Mansell's Williams to win by 0.014 seconds – equivalent to a distance of less than a metre.

Scalextric's other Formula 1 car was the Williams Honda FW11 that Mansell was driving in his battle with Senna. The car almost won him the world title, despite the fact that Nelson Piquet regarded himself as the team's No. 1 driver. Mansell was sitting in third place in Adelaide, which would have earned him enough points to take the championship, when his left rear tyre blew out at almost 200 mph and he had to use every ounce of his strength and skill to manoeuvre the car down the escape road as the Williams scraped the ground, scrabbled for grip and scraped the ground again. His five Grand Prix wins along with Nelson Piquet's four were enough to win the Constructors' Cup for Williams, although there was little rejoicing in the

Williams camp, as Frank Williams had himself been involved in a car crash that year. Driving a hire car near Le Castellet in France, where the team was testing the FW11, Frank had a serious accident which left him paralysed and wheelchair-bound. Four months later, at the British Grand Prix at Brands Hatch, Frank was back in the pits and back in charge, determined not to let his handicap become his team's handicap. The team rewarded him with a 1-2 victory in front of the home crowd.

The First American Invasion

There were more new paint jobs for 1987, with yet another two new versions of the XR3i, including one based on the car driven by Britain's Radio One DJ and TV personality Mike Smith. The flashiest customised paintwork on a car really has to be American though, doesn't it? The golden firebird emblem adorning the bonnet of the new-for-87

Right KITT from the Knightrider TV series with the ghost of an old Datsun in the background

Pontiac Firebird was just about as flash a graphic as they come. The big American coupé had been around for a number of years in a number of different guises. The Americans could always teach the Europeans a thing or two about building engines big and keeping the power output high. Their propensity for producing cars as long and as wide as the QE2, however, meant that they needed big engines, and the Trans-Am/Firebird series could accommodate V8 powerplants of up to around 7 litres. The big motors of the American muscle cars were thirsty beasts, and demanded more regular drink stops than Dean Martin on a hot day. The tank was usually big enough to haul you from one gas station to the next, and with all that power on tap, it certainly didn't take long to get there.

The kind of badge engineering which had allowed the MG octagon to appear on the Metro and Maestro had been rife for years in America, and

trying to tell the difference between a Chevrolet Camaro and a Pontiac Trans-Am/Firebird could sometimes be like holding up two feathers and trying to decide which one you had just accidentally plucked out of Sitting Bull's headdress. Either way you were odds on for a scalping.

It was slightly less difficult to pinpoint the origins of Scalextric's Firebird, despite its lack of feathers, as two of the new sets on offer featured KITT, the famous talking Pontiac from the *Knightrider* TV series. In the show the incredibly clever KITT (Knight Industries Two Thousand) is loaded with on-board computers and can communicate electronically with other computer entities as well as talk to his driver. KITT was ultimately dragged into so much trouble by his driver, crimefighting adventurer Michael Knight (played by David Hasselhoff), that he answered an ad in *Heroes Weekly* and got Hasselhoff a job as a lifeguard.

The Scalextric KITT was teamed up with the villainous Datsun 260Z in the Pursuit Mode figure-of-eight set and the Turbo Boost extended figure-of-eight flying leap set.

The Ferrari 312 T model reappeared in the guise of the 'Stone Avionics' and 'Deserra Sports' cars with 'less elaborate decoration schemes to suit less well-equipped pockets' in the 87 catalogue, but it was another Ferrari model that really stole the limelight – the glorious GTO.

Almost identical to the 308 GTB but with a slightly longer wheelbase, Ferrari announced the twin-turbo 288 GTO at the Geneva motor show, and sports car enthusiasts (with deep pockets) immediately started placing orders. The car was only intended for a production run of 200 to qualify as a Group B racer, but Ferrari eventually decided against racing it. In the end 272 GTOs were produced. The road car had a top speed of around 190 mph and could reach 60 mph from rest in a tyre-scorching 4.5 seconds.

The GTO may never have raced in earnest but the lookalike 308 GTB, which had been around since the mid-Seventies, was a familiar sight sweeping around racetracks all over the world and was even fielded by a number of teams, often with Ferrari's support, as a rally car. With a 2.9-litre V8 engine and body panels fabricated mainly from glass fibre, the 308 was an awesome sight on the European rally circuit, winning the Targa Florio, Quattro Regione, Ypres Rally and Tour de France in 1981. Its GTO stablemate was the highest-priced rally car available from Scalextric in 1987 at over £15, making it an expensive plaything, although not quite as expensive a plaything as a real GTO. Production of the real car ended in 1986, and acquiring one nowadays can cost in excess of £190,000.

The GTO, then, was for serious racers only, and so was a totally new Scalextric development – the SRS cars. SRS (Super Racing System) was designed with competitive racing fiends in mind. The Spanish-produced cars could be taken apart and rebuilt to suit a particular circuit. In effect, you could 'set up' the models just like real racing cars. The bodywork was easily detachable to give access to the chassis, where the skill and judgement of the racer came into play. You could select from three different rear axles, each with a different-sized drive gear which might give faster acceleration out of corners on a twisting track or a higher top speed on a faster circuit. You could even adjust the length of the chassis for optimum performance. Soft rubber tyres gave exceptional grip, aided by a magnet in front of the rear axle to help the car cling to its slot.

Four different SRS cars were available.

Left Lights ablaze, except for the Lotus, the cover of the 1988 catalogue looked truly realistic, except for the Lotus

Right The Ferrari GTO, a rich man's plaything even in Scalextric form

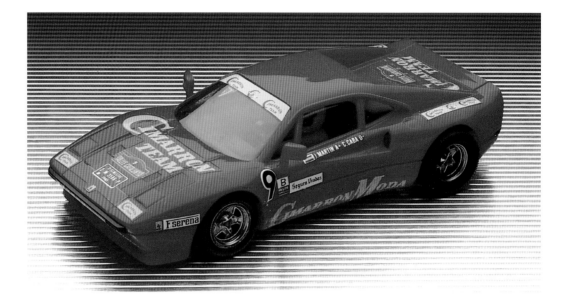

There were two World Sports Car Championship contenders, the Ferrari-powered Lancia LC2 which had finished in sixth and seventh place at Le Mans in 1985; and the Porsche 956 which had filled the top three spots at Le Mans in 1982, top eight places in 1983, top seven places in 1984 (with only a solitary LC2 stopping Porsche repeating their 1983 result), and only the two Lancias spoiling top eight Porsche placings (albeit three of them Porsche 962Cs) in 1985.

The Lancia and the Porsche were joined by the Mercedes 190 E saloon racer, with the Cosworth-tweaked engine that made it a formidable opponent in touring car events, and the outrageous Peugeot 205 Turbo 16. With its 500 horsepower and four-wheel drive, this was the car which helped to end the Quattro's domination of international rallying.

The Peugeot was a Group B racer, like the Metro 6R4, and – also like the 6R4 – it would fall foul of the incoming revisions to the rallying regulations covering Group B cars. A revised Computervision 6R4 appeared with all of the correct aerodynamic add-ons in the 87 catalogue, but it never went into production, probably due in no small part to the demise of the real car.

So passed Scalextric's thirtieth birthday. In the three decades since that memorable toy fair in Harrogate, the company had grown to become a major international manufacturer and carried on racing through more hazards than a Super Stox derby in a breaker's yard. Scalextric France was now no more, but the Spanish operation was still going strong for the time being, and in the United States Scalextric continued to turn over at full revs while many of its biggest competitors had run out of gas. The rise of the computer game had spilt oil on the track for a while, and the ever more sophisticated graphics packages and gaming options reaching the marketplace would continue to pose a problem, but there was now good reason for renewed confidence, with some impressive innovations in the pipeline.

Superheroes were back on song in 1988, as Scalextric battled against the forces of evil with two new sets featuring Matt Trakker and the MASK special agents up against the villainous VENOM scoundrels. Not to be confused with the Jim Carrey film *The Mask*, these fictional organisations were a kids' licensing phenomenon, and the Scalextric contribution came in the form of the MASK Thunderhawk and VENOM Manta cars – both Pontiac Firebird models.

KITT and Knightrider sets continued to be available, but the real superheroes of 1988 were the World Sports Car Championship Jaguar XJR-8 (identified in the catalogue as an XJ8) and Porsche 962C (billed in the catalogue as a 963).

The first of the new breed of mid-engined Jaguar endurance racers was built and campaigned by Bob Tullius' Group 44 outfit in the United States. The Virginia-based company kept Jaguar at the forefront of top-flight prototype racing until Jaguar finally took over and launched an all-out assault on the World Sports Car Championship in 1986. A year later, thanks in no small part to Group 44, the XJR-8 won eight of the ten races in the season. Jaguar became WSC Champions for the

first time and works driver Raul Boesel became World Champion driver. The only fly in the ointment was the fact that the race they most wanted to win was one of the two they lost – Le Mans.

The ointment-smeared fly that denied Jaguar their coveted Le Mans win was Porsche-shaped – the 962C. Porsche had made themselves quite at home at Le Mans over the past few years, losing only twice in the last decade, with most of their wins multiple-placement Blitzkriegs. The 962C's 3-litre turbocharged engine proved more than a match for the Jaguar at Le Mans as the cars thundered on through the 24-hour race at speeds of around 230 mph. Indeed, the Le Mans cars were now so fast that in 1987 the Dunlop chicane was installed to force their speed down as they passed under the famous Dunlop bridge.

The 962C wasn't the only new turbo on offer from Scalextric in 88. The Lotus Honda Turbo, based on the Lotus 99T, was the new Formula 1 car, this year abandoning the black

Above Scalextric's version of Jaguar's championship winning XJR-9

Left The Porsche 962C dripping with ointment

and gold John Player Special (adapted) livery that had almost become Lotus's trademark. Instead, the 99T that Ayrton Senna drove to victory in Detroit and at Monaco was resplendent in the bright yellow and blue colours of Camel cigarettes. Naturally, the Camel name was deleted from the Scalextric version but, strangely, the blue-silhouetted Camel logo was allowed to stay.

No one was paying much attention to the logos anyway (if they did they would spot that the special new tyres on the 99T, Williams FW11 and Lotus 98T were all painted with authentic 'Goodyear Eagle' markings), because the new Lotus had a particularly eye-catching new feature. Since the advent of the turbocharger in Formula 1, pioneered by the Renault RS01 in 1977, the sight of a flame flaring at the rear of a car as it slowed down and unspent fuel burned off from the turbo had become commonplace. On the Scalextric Lotus 99T there was a 'Turboflash' light at the back which simulated the turbo flare when you suddenly released the throttle. Things had

Right The Lotus 99T driven by a creature with a head the size of a pumpkin

Left The creature in the Lotus 98T
that he traded in for the
snazzy new yellow job

certainly come on a bit since the simple tin-plate Maserati and Ferrari thirty years ago.

Another feature fitted to the new yellow Lotus was 'Magnatraction'. This was a development of the STS magnet system. A non-conductive magnet was fitted below the car to keep it glued to the guide rails. This allowed for much faster cornering, but the strength of the magnet would only hold the car for so long. When it did eventually break away you were going off big-time. For those who preferred to show off powersliding around corners, the magnet was easily removed.

With the Lotus 99T, the 98T and Williams FW11 also benefited from Turboflash and Magnatraction.

The good old Porsche 935 was given Magnatraction for 1988, along with a less exciting but even more realistic use of the Turboflash. There was no burn-off flame here but, instead, working brake lights that blinked on when you released the throttle. Now reading that on paper might

leave you totally underwhelmed, or even bring the words 'big' and 'deal' to mind. Remember, though, that authenticity and realism in Scalextric cars has always fuelled the imagination and added enormously to the fun. Remember that and remind yourself of it every time the hairy wart of cynicism starts to curl your lip. In fact, perhaps Scalextric can teach us all a precious lesson here about basic attitudes to life as we negotiate the rocky road of mortality . . . OK, so that last bit's taking it too far, right?

A whole clutch of new models for 88 were fully illuminated, with both head and tail lights, and the Jaguar and Porsche 962C both had similar set-ups to the 935. Only one other car was announced with Magnatraction and brake lights, the Lancia Delta. The new model was based on the Lancia Delta HF 4WD rather than its Group B Delta S4 predecessor. The Delta destroyed the opposition in the 1987 rally season to win Lancia the manufacturers' trophy, make Dario Cerrato European Champion and Juha Kankkunen World Champion. Sadly, the Lancia never made it into production in Scalextric form, for reasons connected with low orders, general production problems and the awkward look of the scaled-down version.

The final new car in 1988, apart from the Ferrari and McLaren Formula 1 cars which joined the SRS range, was the Ford RS200. The RS200 was Ford's Group B rally package, and the only thing it had in common with a production Ford was the windscreen, which came from a Sierra. With its turbocharged 450-horsepower engine mounted

behind the crew, four-wheel drive which could be reduced to just rear-wheel drive, and a compact, pretty design, the RS200 deserved to do far better than it did in international rallies. Unfortunately, it came along just as the Group B cars were outlawed.

Unlike the normally aspirated Metro 6R4, which was raced in domestic rallies after the international ban, the turbocharger of the RS200 meant that it was also excluded from most national rallies. The majority of its racing career was, therefore, to be played out in rallycross events.

Like the Audi Quattro, Scalextric's RS200 had rubber-band four-wheel drive.

Potent Porsches & Fiddly Ferraris

Newcomers to the Scalextric paddock for 1989 were the Ferrari F1/87, the Sierra Cosworth and the Porsche 959.

The Ferrari was a rendition of the car in which Gerhard Berger won in Japan and Australia in 1987. If just two outright wins in a season seems a little meagre for the mighty Maranello team, they

Right Arnold Smalltodge, Northern Area Sales Rep for Jammy Rascal Biscuits, takes delivery of his new Ford Sierra

Right Even Cher had less cosmetic surgery than the Cossie would have facelifts during its Scalextric career

were certainly glad to have them. Ferrari were descending slowly into a long lean period. They hadn't produced a World Champion driver since Jody Scheckter in 1979, and it would be a further 13 years before they came up with another. They had last won the Constructors' Cup four years before, but they wouldn't be tucking it into the trophy cabinet until 1999.

Ferrari's problems were manifold, and on the Scalextric track too their car proved troublesome. Accurately modelled on the F1/87, the Scalextric car had a totally authentic-looking front wing set low on the nose cone. Too low, in fact. The car was asterisked in the catalogue with a footnote explaining that it was 'not suitable for use on Scalextric banked curves'.

Fords have always been involved in Touring Car or TT racing, whether officially or not, and in 1985 the Ford Sierra started to make its presence felt on the track. Andy Rouse, who had won the British Touring Car Championship in 1984 in his Rover Vitesse, stormed to victory in 9 of the 11 rounds of the 1985 championship in his Ford Sierra Cosworth Turbo. The biplane wing on the 'Cossie' made it look remarkably similar to the old XR4i (Hooray! At last Scalextric could put all the work that had gone into the cancelled XR4i to good use!), but the similarities between the two cars were really only skin-deep.

The turbo engine in the RS500 Cossie produced, as its designation strongly hints, 500 horsepower. In 1988 those 500 horses were enough to bring Andy Rouse another 9 wins in the 11 rounds, although he failed to win the BTCC that year because Frank Synter, racing a BMW M3 in a different class section of the championship, won all of his races.

In 1990 the Cossie was back on top, with Robb Gravett taking the BTCC title in his RS500. The Sierra Cosworth also went rallying, but met with only patchy success. It needed four-wheel drive to compete with the big boys, and by the time it got it in 1990 the Sierra was struggling to keep up with the pace of change on the rally scene. As a track racer, however, Ford's saloon seldom failed to impress, winning an unprecedented 40 consecutive races in the BTCC between 1987 and 1990.

With the whole world jumping on the Group B bandwagon to race the most wildly powerful cars they could come up with, Porsche didn't see why they should be left out. The Porsche 959 had a twin-turbo engine that churned out between 450 and 600 horsepower. The German autobahn burner had a top speed of around 190 mph and could hit 60 mph from rest faster than you could say 'Geschwindigkeitsbeschrenkung'. Much faster. A little under four seconds, in fact.

Wins in the Pharaohs Rally in 1985 and the Paris–Dakar in 1986 proved that the 959 was more than just a sprinter, and a Group B class win at Le Mans showed that it had the mettle of a true Porsche. It didn't have the magnet of a Ford, though. The Scalextric Cossie had headlights, brake lights and Magnatraction, while the Porsche came equipped only with head and tail lights.

And as the tail lights of the 1980s fade into the darkness of time, we move with heavy handed motoring metaphor on to the 1990s and some of the most exciting models Scalextric have ever produced.

Below Shinier than a slaphead's bonce, this RS200 had been chrome plated for no other reason than it looked good

Digital Devices and Smokin' Slicks

Right No, you're not swerving to avoid the gap. This manually operated pit stop lane would have a straight section in place when part of a circuit

The range of accessories available going into the 1980s continued the steady build-up of track sections and add-on extras that had been slowly accumulating during the previous few years. Many of the items that had been appearing were, of course, simply reincarnated versions of equipment that had been issued in the 1960s but which had gone out of production during the leaner years.

Two old favourites made a welcome return in the 1980 catalogue. The first was the two-lane pit-stop with the little red buttons on the track which you used to 'switch the points' and bring your car into the pit-lane for urgent repairs. The second was the infamous Right Angle Crossing junction, the accident black spot that was probably the reason why your car had to go into the pits for urgent repairs in the first place.

It was the Speedmaster comic-book hero who really brought Scalextric into the computer age as

Right The Right Angle Crossing – an accident black spot

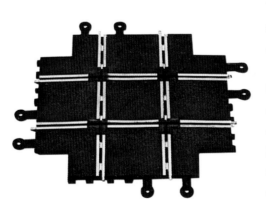

he presented the Think Tank, Fuel Tank and Sound Track systems, helpfully informing the reader in his speech balloon, 'Now you can have your own home computers to help you win!'

Quite how the Sound Track was supposed to help you win was surely only apparent to two-dimensional costume characters, but it was certainly designed for maximum entertainment value. If the breathless catalogue blurb was to be believed, you would be able to hear tyre squeals and gear changes before 'suddenly you hear the telltale skid followed by a disastrous crash indicating that your

Right These computers helped you keep track of your race and were adapted from hardware salvaged from the crashed spaceship of the creature with the pumpkin head

Above The Dunlop Bridge and control tower **(right)** made a welcome return in 1981

opponent has spun off the track in his endeavours to catch you.' It seemed that this little box of tricks gave you almost every sound bar the curses of the driver as he was shunted off the track in a chicane. Nothing's ever as good as the sales material tells you, but realistic racing noises always added to the drama of a big event, and this was a far more sophisticated way of achieving that drama than playing a record of engine sounds or the truly irritating Twin Auto Screams of the 1960s.

Another Sixties gadget was revisited with electronic aid as the Fuel Tank took on the role of the old Fuel Load Gauge. Fuel Tank would calculate how fast you were using up fuel depending on how fast you were driving and how fiercely you were accelerating. Just like the old Fuel Load Guage, as well, it would cut your engine dead if you ran out of fuel. All of which meant that, as Scalextric advised, you had to develop 'a proper strategic race plan, taking into account the circuit together with your car and its performance.'

The Think Tank could be used, like Fuel Tank and Sound Track, in conjunction with the other two computers or independently. This was the electronic version of the old cardboard disc Speed Computer and could be programmed with the length of your circuit to provide digital readouts on average speed, fastest lap time or fastest lap speed, and could time your races over a set period or number of laps.

Using all three computer units together, you had more buttons to push and readouts to monitor than NASA's mission control. Obviously you couldn't do that while concentrating on a race, so now you needed a pit crew to relay all this vital information to you.

All that meant it could get quite crowded around the modern Scalextric track, especially since there was another new building now available. The old control tower was reintroduced in 1981, along with some other old friends, the Dunlop Bridge and Goodwood Chicane. And if the Goodwood Chicane with its straw bales, fencing, traffic cones, embankment and solid wall weren't enough to catch you out then the curved chicane track section also made a comeback. Keeping your car on the track and in one piece hadn't been so difficult for years.

Flicking the tail of your car out as you went round a corner far faster than you really ought to looked quite flash until you came a cropper when the rear wheels slid off the edge of the track. New sets of track borders were introduced to try to keep show-offs on the straight and narrow, but it seemed a fairly futile gesture when the next new development in tricky track sections came along.

In 1982 the Daredevil Loop-the-Loop had swooning Scalextric purists reaching for their smelling salts. Surely this wasn't what model motor racing was all about? You'd never see one of these at Silverstone or Sebring. Who cares? This was a fun piece of kit, and required a fair amount of skill on the part of the racer to negotiate it successfully. You had to hit the base of the loop at a high enough speed for centrifugal force to keep your car on the track as it went up and over, otherwise you would slide back

Above Kamikaze spectators wait to meet their doom at the Goodwood chicane

Below Track borders stopped show-offs churning up carpet fluff

or drop off onto your roof. Also known as the Speed Loop, it took up a lot of space. In order to build up enough speed, it was recommended that you had four or five straight sections of track before the loop, and three after it in order to slow down again.

Certain cars, and the trucks, had to miss out, as there was no way they were fast enough to negotiate the speed loop successfully, but for the faster cars it represented the first-ever opportunity to drive on a Scalextric track upside down without going to Australia. In Australia, of course, they now had the chance to drive the right way up at last, albeit only for a couple of track sections.

Yet another old chum was back again in 1984, as a special set was marketed featuring Blow Out. This was a slightly different version of Blow Out than had been previously available, as this one was presented almost as a children's game, like

Above Pump action Blow Out activator

Kerplunk, Pop Up Pirate or Buckaroo. The track was a simple oval with banked curves at either end around which you raced a pair of Metros. Attached to the track, however, were a couple of pump devices which worked just like the sort of footpump used for blowing up inflatable mattresses or floating toys. Push down on the rubber diaphragm and a paddle in the track flipped up to scupper your rival's car or, as the catalogue copy indelicately put it, 'Hit the ball and give your opponent a blowout.'

Blow Out was intended as just the sort of gift the kids could play with all over Christmas, but what could you give the more serious Scalextric racer? The answer was the Scalextric Gift Pack. The pack included a Dunlop Bridge, Humpback Bridge, straight track sections, lap counter, crash barriers, painted figures and sundry other goodies. Enough, in fact, to keep the recipient busy rebuilding his track long enough for everyone else to enjoy the Christmas TV Bond movie in peace.

Actually, dismantling and rebuilding the track couldn't have been easier, as by now there was a new booklet to buy called *27 Circuits for Scalextric Model Motor Racing*. Although unlikely to outsell a Jackie Collins novel, it had just as much of a plot, with more twists and turns than a snake in a tumble-drier in the back of a Metro doing the Daredevil Loop-the-Loop. How else could you fit in the booklet's 'most exotic layout' of almost 45 feet of track in an overall space of just 8 feet by 4 feet?

By 1986 you could watch a race that was looking more and more authentic with the trackside buildings, pit-stops and spectators, and hear the evocative motor-racing noise with the Sound Track. The only thing missing was the smell of burning oil. Not any more. Now your cars could rev up on a special Rev Start starting grid that let

leap featured chevroned gates on the landing side of the jump to guide the flying Rover and BMW CSL back into their slots. It was still a tricky piece of track to negotiate, though, as was the new Rough Terrain section. The centre of the Rough Terrain straight harboured a series of knobbly humps which could be swivelled (much like the boulder in the James Bond set which activated the ejector seat) to vary the degree of 'roughness' they provided. All in all, it was like driving over a rutted track, and ideal for adding an extra challenge for rally cars.

them spin their wheels on rollers that meant you could squeeze that throttle trigger for all you were worth without actually going anywhere. Oil was injected into a reservoir under the track to produce a cloud of billowing smoke before you pressed a button to retract the rollers and the cars shot off down the track together. The only problem with the new gimmick was if your mum caught a whiff of it and phoned the fire brigade.

New gimmicks aside, the successful trend for the reintroduction of old ideas forged ever onwards with the new Flying Leap set in 1987. Far simpler and less hazardous than the old version, the new

More devices of an electronic nature were on offer in 1988 with a new lap recorder incorporated into the top of a paddock-style building. Like previous versions, it notched up a lap each time a car passed over its special track section and this version displayed an LED readout on the rooftop lap 'scoreboard'. The new lap-counter building came complete with two extra straight track sections, two pit-stop buildings, pit-crew figures and enough barriers and flags to stage a walkabout by the Queen.

The LEDs were in action again on the Hazard Long Chicane. Chicanes had long been a popular feature on Scalextric circuits, and this one had all of the traffic cones, barriers and flags you would

Above left Blow Out . . . er . . . Blowing Out

Left Bedtime reading for budding circuit builders

Above The Scalextric gift pack

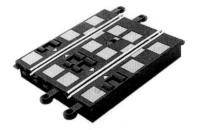

Above How the Rev Start starting grid looks before it goes up in smoke

expect if the Queen gave up her walkabout and decided to have a go in an XR3i. It also featured a series of flashing warning lights which, no doubt, Her Majesty would take to be a welcoming salute and speed on into the hazard. The resulting turmoil might well dent her tiara a bit and leave Prince Charles thinking that he might get to have a go on the throne after all.

The old Auto Start idea was another to be given a revamp, with the introduction of the Start Light Gantry. The lighting gantry straddled the track and the different lights represented a period for practice, which could then be reset to show flashing lights tracking towards the centre of the gantry before the red lights changed to green and you were off. Used in conjunction with the Rev Start starting grid, you could now have all the smoke and light effects of either a Formula 1 race, an Indy Car event or a Pink Floyd concert.

Determined to regain all of the ground lost since the early Seventies, yet more ideas resurfaced from the Scalextric archives to make a welcome

appearance towards the end of the Eighties. 'Race Tuned' cars had been an early Scalextric innovation, and now the name was revived for a series of special accessories to help you customise your cars and optimise your highly honed driving skills. The Race Tuned hand throttle was described as giving 'a split-second edge', perhaps just enough to beat the Queen into the illuminated chicane, and the range of axles, bearings and other ancillaries were all designed to give you the chance to customise your car to your own preference as well as to 'set up' your car for a particular circuit.

Above The Rough Terrain Track simulated driving on an inner city bus route

Below Go take a Flying Leap! Too much fun ever to go out of fashion

Below Public Address System for race announcements or, with the microphone in a thick sock, Darth Vader impressions

Left The new digital lap counter for 1988 came with a row of paddock buildings and figures practising Tai Chi

Left The fantastic gantry-mounted lights of the Start Light Post

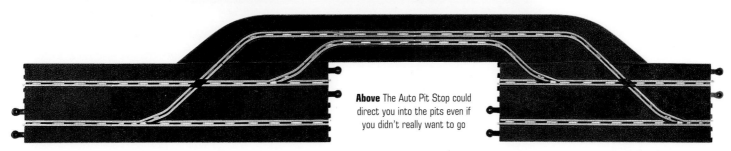

Above The Auto Pit Stop could direct you into the pits even if you didn't really want to go

Below Accessories either provided 'more show' or 'more go'. The syringe provided 'more show' by feeding oil to produce smoke in the Rev Start starting grid

The final forgotten hero to make its return was the Public Address System. The new system was battery operated and designed to fit unobtrusively inside the recent control tower and grandstand buildings.

The ultimate announcement to boom out over the new PA as the Eighties drew to a close must surely have been: 'So ends another decade of Scalextric racing, but there's much more to come in the Nineties so, whatever age you are, for goodness sake don't grow up yet!'

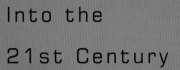

Into the
21st Century

Into the 21st Century

Waving the chequered flag in early 1990 to call a halt to the day's Scalextric racing on the set that had been the focus of attention since Christmas was more than likely to produce a response of 'Eat my shorts!' or 'Don't have a cow, man!' Sometimes dads can be so embarrassing.

Bart Simpson's catchphrases had been subverting the vocabulary of impressionable youth (and their impressionable elders) since the broadcast of the first episode of *The Simpsons* just before Christmas 1989. Bart would no doubt have loved to have a Scalextric set, but Homer would almost certainly have hogged the hand controls.

The new cars Homer could have been racing in 1990 included the Sauber Mercedes C9, the BMW M3, the Benetton-Ford B189 and the Tyrrell 018.

A former garage owner and racing driver turned sports prototype constructor, Swiss-born Peter Sauber had been building experience and skills in his racing team with their Mercedes-engined cars until 1989, when they showed Jaguar and Porsche that Mercedes was truly back in the game by taking first and second places at Le Mans. The World Sports Car Championship Constructors' title and drivers' title went to Sauber and their man Jean-Louis Schlesser. The following year Mercedes threw their full weight behind Sauber, and the V8,

5-litre, turbocharged C9s thundered home in first place in eight of the nine championship races, with only the Le Mans laurels eluding them.

The C9 earned its place alongside the reliveried Porsche 962C and the Jaguar which had been redecorated as the XJR-9, although the Sauber Mercedes was campaigned in just one further season, when it did not fare so well. Sauber Mercedes, of course, then set their sights on Formula 1.

The Formula 1 stars in Scalextric's 1990 line-up included the Benetton B189, actually looking suspiciously more like a B188, but let's not be too picky. The B189 brought Benetton a victory in Japan when Alessandro Nannini won at Suzuka. This was only Benetton's second-ever win – the first came three years earlier in Mexico City when Gerhard

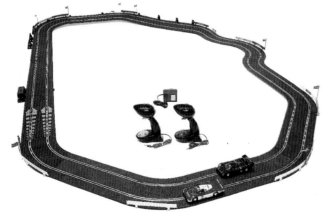

Below This set came complete with Mega Sound hand controls, yet another racing-noise device

Berger triumphed. One of Benetton's sponsors was Camel cigarettes and, while the Camel name is absent from the Scalextric car, that old blue camel silhouette still manages to put in an appearance on the model photographed for the catalogue.

The same camel, or perhaps a larger relative, also shows up on the Tyrrell 018 in the catalogue photograph, although it never made it onto all of the production models of either car. The Tyrrell and the Benetton had more in common than the humpy old 'ship of the desert', though. Both were powered by the ubiquitous Ford Cosworth V8 and neither posed a major threat to the leading teams of the day. The Tyrrell was far from being an unworthy car, however. It showed promising form throughout the season, with some good performances by drivers Jonathan Palmer, Michele Alboreto, Jean Alesi and Johnny

Herbert. Four drivers? Surely a Formula 1 team only fields two cars? That may well be, but Alesi and Herbert were brought in when Alboreto left the team in mid-season. Alboreto had not been happy at Tyrrell for some time, but argued that he was bound to leave because his contract with his personal sponsors, Marlboro, forbade him to drive a car that had that old blue camel on the side.

The BMW M3, meanwhile, had been making quite a name for itself in Touring Car races since 1987 without the aid of a single camel. Announced in 1985, the M3 was ready to race in 1987, whereupon it won the German Touring Car Championship at the hands of the BMW-supported Zakspeed team, while Wilfried Vogt, driving for the Lindner team, won the European Championship. The M3 was also used to good effect in rallying,

Left The BMW M3 was a teutonic masterpiece, as successful a racing car as it was a street-cruising mobile ghetto blaster

Right The McLaren-Honda MP4/4 took the chequered flag on the cover of the 1990 catalogue, but it never left the paddock as a Scalextric racer

Championships. By 1990, Roberto Ravaglia had taken the Italian title on five consecutive occasions in a BMW M3.

The list of drivers and teams that have campaigned the M3 could go on for as long as the car's impressive career. It was still winning championships right up to its 'retirement' in 1992, two years after the last of the 'old' 3 Series road cars had rolled off the production line and the new 3 Series M3 was about to take over. Although the M3 was fielded in Group A, the class for cars that are as close as possible to normal production cars, a racing M3 was a far more aggressive beast than the production M3. The production car was no slouch, though, with up to around 215 horsepower, 150 mph top speed and 0–60 mph in just over six seconds. The racer fielded by BMW specialist team Schnitzer had around 300 horsepower on tap and was as fast as a dachshund on a sausage safari.

when Bernard Beguin stormed to victory in the 1987 Tour de Corse. It was on the track, however, that the various professional teams, racing with the support of the BMW factory, really shone. In fact, the M3 was unstoppable. In 1988 the car won the German, French, British and Italian Touring Car

Batman & the Flying Leap Return

The most impressive car of the 1990 Scalextric show by far, though, was the Batmobile. No, not the BMW CSL with the bookshelf on the bootlid, but the

Right The victim of a licensing agreement that ultimately never happened, the McLaren MP4/4 was withdrawn from sale

Left The Batmobile. No, not another version of the BMW. This really was Batman's car. The caped crusader's rival, the Joker, did have German wheels, though, in the shape of this Porsche **(above)**

real Batmobile, as driven by Michael Keaton in the 1989 movie *Batman*. The Batmobile came in two sets, one of them was a simple figure-of-eight Chase set with banked curves, the other the good old Flying Leap set. In each case Batman's opposite number, the Joker, drove a Porsche. Although the Porsche is undoubtedly a fast car, one has to assume that the real Batmobile would have got the better of it. Apart from its turbine engine, remote central locking which activated an armadillo-like armoured shell, and complete remote-control driving capability, the Batmobile had more offensive and defensive weaponry and gadgets than James Bond could ever have dreamt of. If Speedmaster could only have driven this car, he would have been in superhero seventh heaven.

One car which featured in the 1990 catalogue but had to be withdrawn from sale in the UK was the McLaren-Honda MP4/4. The model was made in Spain for a time, but Scalextric could not strike a licensing agreement with McLaren.

Apart from this unfortunate false start, Scalextric had sprinted into the 1990s faster than Carl Lewis with his pants on fire . . . and that was fast. In 1991 Lewis set a new world record of 9.86 seconds for

the 100m without setting light to his shorts, but even he couldn't keep up with Scalextric's new offering for that year, the Lamborghini Diablo (unless he was driving another Diablo, of course).

Lamborghini's Devil car (Diablo means Devil in Spanish) had a 5.8-litre V12 engine that could whip the Italian thoroughbred up to 60 mph from rest in only 4.2 seconds and take it on to over 200 mph. An exotic car by anyone's standard, the scissor-type doors opened forwards and upwards, the angular styling somehow contriving to make that eccentricity seem perfectly natural. In 1991, the Diablo was given four-wheel drive. You could then take up farming and use your Diablo as a tractor to plough the odd field or two, just like the agricultural machines Ferruccio Lamborghini started out making at the end of World War II. Or maybe not . . .

Left Lamborghini Diablo – the world's fastest tractor?

Right German endurance machines
dominate the cover of the 1991
catalogue in the shape of the Sauber
Mercedes and Porsche 962C

There were no other completely new cars on offer in the 1991 catalogue, although there were plenty of brand spanking new paint jobs decorating some of the well established models from the XR3i to the Porsche 962. In all, 14 cars boasted new liveries, with the Penzoil and Toshiba 'Indy' cars appearing in the guise of a less elaborately finished Renault RS01. 'X' cars also made an appearance, simplified models without lights or any of the modern gimmickry. Intended to be light and fast, they were stripped down for speed and, like the simplified Formula 1 models, they were substantially less expensive than their fully loaded counterparts. Without Magnatraction and the like, you could have a Sierra Cosworth for around £16 in the UK, a saving of over 25 per cent on the price of the better-equipped version.

Right German endurance machines dominate the cover of the 1991 catalogue in the shape of the Sauber Mercedes and Porsche 962C

Sport of Kings & Teenage Turtles

What would you do with the money you saved? Some would say, 'Put it on a horse' and Scalextric gave you just the opportunity in 1991 when the sport of kings took to the slotted track. Unlike the previous Jump Jockey system, the new breed of horses

Below The Le Mans-winning Sauber Mercedes

raced just like the cars, the horse and jockey perched on a curious built-up trolley which housed the motor and ran on four wheels. It was more like racing statues of horses and jockeys than the real thing, but it proved to be a popular departure for Scalextric, although petrolheads would doubtless rather have seen the investment ploughed into more new model cars.

Although there were no new cars, the Scalextric range had now reached the sort of level it hadn't attained for years, with 18 car sets, two motorbike sets, three horse racing sets (Ascot, Newmarket and the Derby) and 61 vehicles available. Some of the sets, it has to be said, were far removed from motor sport. The two Batman sets had been joined by no less than three Teenage Mutant Hero Turtles sets. Cowabunga!

Toy of the year in the UK in 1990, the Teenage Mutant Hero Turtles (in their comic-book form

Left Turtle in a truck –'The Heroes in a Half Shell' added a welcome touch of nonesense to the range in 1991

they were Ninja Turtles, but the reputation of Japanese Ninja warriors as assassins wasn't felt to be a healthy role model for kids when the unprecedented licensing programme got under way) also helped to boost the number of vehicles in the catalogue, as there were no fewer than eight to be collected.

Riding motorised skateboards, Leonardo, Donatello, Raphael and Michelangelo did battle with their evil enemies, who rode on fairly anonymous blocks of plastic that looked suspiciously like the engine units for the racehorse pieces. And if your hunger for Turtles product was even greater than the Turtles' famous appetite for pizza, there were two more vehicles in the shape of a specially decorated Datsun 4x4 with a Turtle standing on the flatbed and a weapons-laden 'Party Wagon' VW camper van, both of which came from the Turtles to the Rescue set.

Left The Turtles also took to the track on skateboards and (below) in their VW 'Party Wagon'

143

Right Lamborghini and Ferrari setting a furious pace on the cover of the 1992 catalogue.

SCALEXTRIC

1:32 SCALE
33rd EDITION

The Datsun and the VW, however, were available outside the set, as were the other Turtles pieces, and could run perfectly well on any normal Scalextric track. That gives rise to the bizarre notion that you could watch a race-prepared 500 horsepower Ford Sierra Cosworth go up against a large green turtle proficient in the martial arts and riding a skateboard powered by what looked like an air-conditioning unit – without consuming any illegal substances.

Those who expected the lack of new cars in 1991 to spawn a rash of desirable models for 1992 were not altogether disappointed. For Formula 1 aficionados, there was the Ferrari 643. The troubles in the Ferrari Formula 1 camp continued through 1991, the year in which they introduced the 643. Alain Prost was forced out of the team, having uttered what Ferrari thought to be undue criticism

of their car in press interviews. Prost may have been right, though. His Ferrari teammate Jean Alesi and the team's test driver, Gianni Morbidelli, who was promoted to replace Prost, struggled to scrape together enough points to push Ferrari up to third in the Constructors' Championship. The 643, then, was not one of Ferrari's most successful cars. Put it on a Scalextric track, however, and it's every bit as good as the rest.

The other Ferrari on offer in Scalextric's 1992 catalogue was based on a car that was more than just as good as the rest – it was outstanding. The Ferrari F40 was intended by the Italian car giant to celebrate its 40th anniversary. Based on the platform of the 288 GTO but with radically redesigned bodywork, the F40 had a GTO engine enlarged to 3 litres which retained the GTO's twin turbos to produce around 480 horsepower (around 680 in racing form) from the V8. The F40 rocketed to 60 mph in 3.9 seconds and had a top speed of 201 mph, making it the fastest Ferrari road car to date when it was launched in 1988, and the fastest production car in the world to boot.

Built like a racing car (fortunately not the 643), there was no need to strip out the inside of the car if

you wanted actually to go racing, but it was quite a responsibility throwing £163,000 worth of car around a racetrack, especially when you consider that only 1,311 were built. It would be like gambling with a piece of history.

Nostalgia for the Nineties

To keep the Ferrari and the Lamborghini company, Scalextric offered its own roadgoing (i.e. stripped of all its sponsors' names and given a nice coat of paint) Porsche 962. You wouldn't really want to cram yourself into the cramped, overheated cockpit of a 962 for a quick trip down to the supermarket for the weekly shopping, but it would certainly get you back home again fast enough to stop the ice cream from melting.

The ice cream, of course, would be to nosh while you sat down to watch BBC television's

Left Ford Escort Cosworths illuminate the cover of the 1993 catalogue

Below The Ferrari 643, not one of the Italian team's finest products

The 'Power and the Glory' cars.
Clockwise from top left, Mini Cooper, Alfa Romeo, Bentley, Ferrari, Tyrrell, Vanwall, BRM, Ferrari P4 and Ford 3L

The Power and the Glory history of the racing car. Scalextric capitalised on the popularity of the TV series by issuing a series of historic racing cars the sight of which delighted slot car fans. 'The Power and the Glory' collection consisted of the Mini Cooper, Ford 3L, Ferrari P4, Tyrrell Ford 007, BRM, Vanwall and the incomparable Bentley and Alfa Romeo. The Bentley and Alfa, while exquisite models, commanded an excruciating price at £30 each, a whopping £13 more than Scalextric's final newcomer for 1992, the Ford Fiesta XR2i.

Baby brother to the Sierra XR4i and Escort XR3i, the Fiesta was ideal material for a 'hot hatch'. For a start, it had a hatch, and with a fuel-injected 1600 cc engine, it was hot. It even managed to maintain that heat in the shade, as it was overshadowed in motor sport by the champion Cossie and the prolific XR3i. With Ford having attempted to send the Fiesta rallying in its early days, everyone quickly realised that the little car had far better prospects on the track and in rallycross, and it was raced in club events with great success for many years.

Not to be outdone by its smaller sibling, the XR3i

was kicked upstairs to join the Sierra Cosworth in 1993, acquiring a new shape and its own version of the Cossie wing into the bargain. The real Escort also quickly showed the XR2i where it had gone wrong in rallying when it took to the rough-and-tumble contests in 1993. With its turbocharged 2-litre engine, seven-speed gearbox and four-wheel drive (it was the Group A car least like the production car on which it was supposed to be based), the Escort Cosworth came second on its debut in the Monte Carlo Rally. There followed wins in the Portuguese, Tour de Corse, Acropolis, San Remo and Catalonia rallies. First and second placings in major international events then became almost monotonously regular occurrences for the Escort Cosworth, with drivers such as François Delecour and Carlos Sainz behind the wheel.

A handful of re-liveried Formula 1 cars made their way into the cheaper price bracket in the 1993 catalogue, but there was one new model, the Minardi M192. Giancarlo Minardi had entered Formula 1 via Formula 3 and Formula 2 in 1985. It would be three years before they even scored a point in the championship, but such was Minardi's passion for motor sport that he kept the team going despite financial hardship and little reward in the way of results. The M192 is based on the car in which Christian Fittipaldi managed to snatch fifth place in Japan and earn himself his first-ever Grand Prix point. Powered by a Lamborghini engine which proved too temperamental for the Minardi team, the car was hopelessly unreliable, and there was little else for Fittipaldi to celebrate that season.

The Scalextric Minardi is really just a revised version of the Scalextric Ferrari 643, but the two cars

were so similar in real life that without their distinctive colours most people could never have told them apart.

The only other new Scalextric car to appear that year was the remarkable Jaguar XJ220. Announced at the 1988 Birmingham Motor Show, it surfed a wave of prosperity and confidence that saw the projected production run sell out in advance orders within days. The orders were placed, however, not just by lovers of fast cars but also by speculators who hoped to be able to turn a profit by selling either the finished car or their place in the queue to receive a finished car.

When the new car finally started to find its way into the hands of the buyers, it fulfilled the speed fiends' wildest dreams. The 3.5-litre (Jaguar's trusty 5.3-litre V12 was deemed too bulky) twin-turbo V6 whistled up to 60 mph in only 3.5 seconds and the car really could do 220 mph. It was the fastest road car Jaguar had ever built and, at the time, the fastest road car in the world.

A strictly limited production run of 350 cars was completed, but the cream of the Big Cats had a sour aftertaste. There were rapid changes in the market for exotic cars while the XJ220 was being built, and when some people realised that they would not be able to sell their new car on for a handsome profit – which they would truly need as the XJ220 cost £403,000 – they tried to back out of their contracts and some nasty legal proceedings ensued.

Now, with the XJ220, Lamborghini Diablo and Ferrari F40, Scalextric had the world's fastest,

Above The Ford Fiesta, hatched and hot it had both the qualifications to become a Hot Hatch

Below The Ferrari F40. Even in Scalextric form it looked like it was doing 100 mph while standing still

North American Contour or Mercury Mystique. The cars were built in Kansas City and Genk in Belgium with parts sourced from all over the world. Sales of the US models fell some way below expectations but in Europe the car became a massive success, which only goes to prove that the gulf between American and European tastes in motor cars is every bit as wide as the Atlantic.

The Mondeo's popularity in Europe and the UK as a family and business car and general workhorse was reflected on the racetrack, where the V6 Cosworth Mondeo attempted to pick up where the Sierra Cosworth had left off. The cars certainly impressed with their pace when they joined the British Touring Car Championship midway through the 1993 season, but competition in the series was tougher than ever. The V6 Cossie was up against the formidable BMW 318i and later the Alfa 155 and Vauxhall/Opel Vectra. Nevertheless, the car put up some sterling performances at the hands of Paul Radisich, pulling off three wins and ending the season third in the Drivers' Championship. The following year New Zealander Radisich won the FIA

most exclusive road cars in its stable.

Where do you go from the world's most exclusive? Why, the world's most commonplace, naturally. What was the most commonplace car imaginable in 1994? Why, the travelling sales reps' carriage, the Ford Mondeo, naturally. Launched in early 1993, the Sierra replacement was conceived by Ford as a 'world car' to be sold in Europe as the Mondeo and in the US as the

Left F40, Diablo and an outrageous roadgoing (or slotted-track-going) Porsche 962C

Touring Car World Cup and a special 20-lap touring car race at Donington. The first of the Scalextric Mondeos was pictured in the catalogue with Radisich's name featuring prominently on the rear side window.

As if stealing the Mondeo's thunder on the racetrack wasn't enough, the BMW 318i also turned up in Scalextric form in 1994. Tim Harvey had won the British Touring Car Championship in a 318i in 1992, but the Scalextric car was based on the cars raced by Team Schnitzer on behalf of BMW, with their distinctive 'chequered flag' rear end. The model that appeared in the 1994 catalogue bore the number 22, identifying it as being based on the car in which Jo Winkelhock won the British Touring Car Championship in 1993 with teammate Steve Soper coming second. Winkelhock became the first non-Briton to capture the title in over ten years.

Around the world, the car was no less successful. In Germany Johnny Cecotto won the new Warsteiner-ADC-GT-Cup and Dieter Quester became Austrian National Champion. Hillclimb championships all over Europe tumbled like

ninepins to the all-conquering BMWs, and Roberto Ravaglia switched to a 318i to win the Italian Touring Car Championship yet again. The 3 series would go on to remain competitive for many years, Jo Winkelhock winning the German Super Touring

Left The new Jaguar XJ220 takes on the Diablo in what looks like a reversing contest on the 1994 catalogue

Right The XJ220 drives the F40 round the bend

Championship in 1995 and the Australian version of the tournament falling to Paul Morris's 3 series in 1997 as the 3 series continued to mature.

The year 1994 also saw the return of the Racing Trucks, with Silkolene and Bardahl liveries and improved performance, thanks in no small way to the addition of Magnatraction. The Sierra Cosworth was decked out in Police paintwork and the Mini Cooper, Metro 6R4 and Escort Cosworth were among the others to benefit from new racing colours.

On the Formula 1 front the Williams Renault FW15C was announced but kept under wraps,

literally photographed under a sheet for the catalogue, as the team's new sponsorship wasn't announced in time to catch the printing. The car eventually appeared in the blue, white and gold Rothmans colours (suitably amended) more readily associated with the FW16 in which Damon Hill won the British Grand Prix, one of his six victories in 1994. Sadly, the FW16 was also the car in which the great Ayrton Senna died in a tragic accident while leading the field at Imola.

The other Formula 1 car for 1994 was the Benetton B193, as driven by rising star Michael Schumacher in 1993. A series of strong finishes for Schumacher was topped by his second Grand Prix win, which came in Portugal as a result of an very quick pit-stop. The pit crew were fast gaining a reputation for their speedy turnaround of cars during races, and at Estoril they worked their magic to buy Schumacher the few precious seconds he needed to snatch the lead from Alain Prost.

Another apparent Formula 1 newcomer was the Dallara 192. Dallara was an Italian racing

Below The Scalextric Mondeo was based on saloon car ace Paul Radisich's car

team with strong Ferrari connections which had been competing in Formula 1 since 1988. The Dallara 192 was powered by Ferrari's Formula 1 engine, and Scalextric took the association one slight step further by representing the car in the form of a repainted Ferrari 643.

Two other cars which received much the same treatment were the Team Omega Securities and Texaco 500 'Indy' cars, which were reworkings of the Tyrrell 018 and Ferrari 643. All of these revised models had Magnatraction and were ideal 'second stream' racers, undercutting the main Formula 1 range in price as a stopgap between the most expensive cars and very basic 'economy' single-seat racers.

The success of the Power and the Glory series prompted three more reissues of older models in 1994 in a special 'Collector Series'. The 25th birthday

Above and below The new BMW 3 series was every bit as successful on the race track as the old cars had been

Left BMW and Ford, dicing on the Scalextric track just as they did in real saloon car races

Right The new Williams Renault FW15C takes the lead on the cover of the 1995 catalogue

Below A Formula I set featuring 1998's Pole Position Sound Control Centre

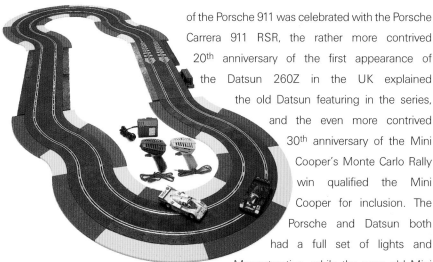

Above The dignity of these normally serious-minded Porsches was severely disturbed when they were asked to spin through 360° in Wild 3 Sixty

Below The Mighty Morphin Power Rangers aboard one of their Battlebikes

of the Porsche 911 was celebrated with the Porsche Carrera 911 RSR, the rather more contrived 20th anniversary of the first appearance of the Datsun 260Z in the UK explained the old Datsun featuring in the series, and the even more contrived 30th anniversary of the Mini Cooper's Monte Carlo Rally win qualified the Mini Cooper for inclusion. The Porsche and Datsun both had a full set of lights and Magnatraction, while the poor old Mini missed out on any such modern refinement.

By the mid-1990s the world was changing faster than Superman in a phone booth. The great communications revolution had succeeded not in saving people time but rather in speeding up the pace at which everything had to be done. A letter that might have taken two days by mail now took two nanoseconds by email and the number of computers in circulation in 1995 was estimated at 222 million – equivalent to more than three each for every single person in the UK.

Fortunately, however, people somehow still managed to make time for old-fashioned leisure pursuits. More than 20 million of them attended NBA basketball games in the US, while the cinema saw ever-increasing box office takings and the return of an old friend – James Bond's Aston Martin DB5. The Pierce Brosnan-flavoured 007 was at the wheel, chasing Xenia Onatopp's Ferrari down a winding Riviera mountain road in the new Bond movie, *Goldeneye*.

If the idea of 007 being involved in a car chase that took in some beautiful mountain scenery gave you something of a sense of *déjà vu*, then one of the new 1995 racing sets from Scalextric would leave you with the very strong impression that you'd had *déjà vu* before.

The two cars in the set were Porsche 962Cs – familiar, yeah, but not overly remarkable. The set, however, was called Wild 3 Sixty, and the cars incorporated a free-spinning guide blade that would allow them to skid through 180° to head back the way they had come, or 360° as if to burn doughnut tyre marks on the track like some Formula 1 show-off. Now that all sounds very familiar, doesn't it? The system had first been used almost 15 years previously on the Super Stox set, followed by the Mini Banger Racing set, but it had never featured such prestigious racing cars as the Porsches. Not for the serious racer, then, but you've got to let your hair down some time, don't you?

Left Alfa Romeo's 155 was beautifully detailed in Scalextric form, right down to the mesh on the driver's side window

More Merchandising Mayhem

Another concept to make a return was that of the licensed children's character product, this time in the shape of the Mighty Morphin Power Rangers Battlebikes, although since the Power Rangers' main talent was their ability to change shape, or morph, you never really knew what to expect. Fortunately, the Power Rangers remained pretty much in one form during their Scalextric missions – motorcycle and sidecar combinations, otherwise known as Battlebikes. It might have been interesting if they could have morphed into a laser-equipped Bentley, or even a sabre-toothed elephant on roller skates, but Battlebikes they remained.

A great deal of morphing was going on in the rest of the Scalextric range for 1995, with the Escort, Mini, Metro, Mondeo, Porsche 911, BMW 318i, Ferrari F40 and Jaguar XJ220 all being treated to new colour schemes.

The vintage Bentley was offered again in 1995, separate from the Power and the Glory series and coloured blue, in a new Racing Classics category along with its old sparring partner the

Alfa Romeo, now in Italian racing red.

That wasn't the only Alfa in the catalogue, either. The touring car field was boosted to the tune of one as the Alfa Romeo 155 joined the starting grid. The Scalextric Alfa was modelled on the striking red (naturally) and white racing colours of the Alfa Romeo works team, specifically the car driven by Gabriele Tarquini in the 1994 British Touring Car Championship. Alfa Corse, the competition arm of Alfa Romeo, launched an all-out assault on the BTCC in 1994 with Giampiero Simoni as teammate to Tarquini in the 155 TS cars.

Simoni came fifth in the championship and Tarquini won outright, stealing the first five races so comprehensively that he was back home eating a plate of spaghetti before most of the others had even finished. In fact, most of the wins were so emphatic that the Alfa's performances brought allegations that its aerodynamic wing and adjustable front air dam were against the competition rules. When the complaints were taken seriously, Alfa withdrew from one race while a resolution was

Right Scalextric Lagunas at pace. Catalogue photography like this was now becoming so realistic that it was often difficult to tell whether or not the cars were the real thing

sought. Despite having missed a race, Tarquini still won the championship.

A few strays from the Formula 1 herd were rounded up and rebranded to complete the 1995 stockholding. Termed 'USA Racers', the Team Eurosport and Team Duracell cars were remodelled Tyrrell 018s with altered tooling, while the 'Formula X' BP and Firehawk cars were actually former Ferrari and Brabham models.

The Incredible Shrinking Set

Déjà vu had been the problem for 1995. One day it probably will be again, but will we remember? The problem in 1996 was that Scalextric looked like it was getting smaller, or was it that you were morphing into something much bigger? No, it was definitely getting smaller. Micro Scalextric had arrived. Keen to keep up with the growing (or should that be expanding shrinking?) market for teensy little slot cars, Hornby Hobbies Ltd – Scalextric's parent company – had licensed the

right to market an American 1:64 scale system called MR1 in 1995. A year later, they were ready to launch their own homegrown system – Micro Scalextric.

Conceived with the younger racer in mind, Micro cars were simple, robust and nicely detailed with a superhesion magnet system similar to Magnatraction and a fair turn of speed. The 1:64 ratio was thought to offer a more user-friendly tabletop size, being half the size of Scalextric, and the construction time from boxed to racing was minimal.

There were six Micro Scalextric sets covering endurance racing, touring cars, two Formula 1 sets, a stunt loop system and a mountain rally set featuring two cute little Vauxhall Fronteras. The range of cars included some from the MR1 system, which was more or less compatible with Micro Scalextric, as well as the Fronteras, Porsche 911, AMG Mercedes, Jaguar XJ220, Alfa 155, Ferrari F40 and Ferrari and McLaren Formula 1 cars.

Zooming back up to twice the size, the 1:32 cars for 1996 included the Alfa 155 in the Old Spice racing colours of the Prodrive team which Alfa Corse had left to contest the BTCC and also in new Martini racing livery, although the word 'Martini' was excised on the Scalextric car. Two new Mondeos and two new BMW 318is also joined the range while the totally new touring car ensemble featured the Renault Laguna, AMG Mercedes C-class and Opel Calibra.

The Scalextric Laguna was based on the car that Alain Menu had been racing for Renault UK in the BTCC since 1994. In their first year Menu and teammate Tim Harvey brought Renault second place in the championship and the following year Menu proved incredibly fast later in the season, coming second in the Drivers' Championship for the second year in a row and combining with new team partner Will Hoy to win the Constructors' trophy for Renault.

The aggressively styled C-class Merc and Opel/Vauxhall Calibras raced in the International Touring Car Championship. Unlike the British contest, the ITCC allowed radical modification of

Left German DTM racing championship power tourers Mercedes C-class and Opel Calibra

Right It's Ford's turn to show how fast they can reverse on the cover of the 1996 catalogue

the production cars, having developed from the DTM German championship where technological innovations were widely encouraged. There were some rules, though, chief among them the limiting of the engine size to 2.5 litres and 6 cylinders with no turbos permitted. Cars like the four-wheel-drive V6 Calibra, the big Mercedes or the four-wheel-drive Alfa 155 V6 could, nevertheless, produce up to 500 horsepower.

Right The Williams Renault FW15C makes another catalogue cover appearance in 1997

Fought over 26 rounds with 12 in Germany, 10 in Europe and further races in Japan and Brazil, the ITCC was contested by only three manufacturers, the aforementioned Mercedes, Alfa and Opel. The whole championship endured for only one season.

The Formula 1 championship proved eminently more durable, and the new Scalextric model for 1996 was the McLaren Mercedes MP4/10. Powered by a V10 3-litre Mercedes engine, the MP4/10 was distinguished by its occasional use of a small 'moustache' wing mounted on top of the engine cover and the equally occasional use of a not-so-small moustachioed driver mounted in front of the engine cover – Nigel Mansell. McLaren were determined to attract a 'star' driver to the team for 1996, and Mansell, in the twilight of his Formula 1 career, was recruited at great expense. He had a problem squeezing in to the cramped cockpit of the McLaren and, having been signed after the car had been developed, he even missed a couple of races while the car was altered to fit him.

Mansell never liked the MP4/10, however, even going as far as describing it in public as undrivable. That pleased neither the powers that be at Mercedes nor McLaren boss Ron Dennis, and it's fair to assume that harsh words were spoken. Mansell duly left the team mid-season and retired from Formula 1. It was far from being the glorious end to a truly remarkable career that he would have wanted, but it would seem he had a point about the car. McLaren had a dismal season with the MP4/10, their worst for 15 years. New driving talent and improved results did, however, lurk just around the corner.

Four renegade Scalextric Formula 1 cars headed for the bargain basement to complete the 1996 line-up, and three more assorted renegades took

Left The McLaren MP4/10 passes the Williams on the outside in a classic Scalextric overtaking manouevre

pole position for the 1997 catalogue, although by now a new one-size-fits-all budget body style for single-seat racers had been introduced on the Team GQ and Team Navico cars. Previous manufacturing agreements with Scalextric's Spanish associate company had come to grief and the Spanish outfit was now a budding competitor, so the new generic racing bodies were produced in China.

Apart from the Chinese connection, there were only two completely new cars in the Scalextric catalogue in 1997, with Sauber and Jordan Formula 1 models joining the Micro Scalextric range. Being half the size, though, they probably only counted as one car.

Although not completely new, the Renault Laguna pulled on a different coat with the racing livery of the Williams Renault team. The Williams Formula 1 organisation had been involved with the touring car championships for a couple of years, and now ran the Renault team. This extended Williams' Formula 1 involvement with Renault, of course, but Formula 1 boss Frank Williams also made clear the high regard in which he held saloon car racing when he was quoted as saying that, 'Next to Formula 1, the British Touring Car Championship is the most important in the world outside America.'

No sooner had Leonardo di Caprio's *Titanic* slipped beneath the waves and the candles been blown out on the *Dandy* comic's 60th birthday cake than we were rushing headlong into 1998, barely aware that Scalextric electric model motor racing was now 40 years old.

Scalextric's touring car stable saw the arrival of a sensational newcomer in 1998 in the Audi A4

Right The Audi A4 was unstoppable in saloon car races all over the world

Quattro. Although they may have been better known for their success on the world's rally circuits, Audi had always maintained a foothold in track racing, with Bob Tullius's Group 4 fielding the Audi 200 Quattro in TransAm races in the late Eighties and Frank Biela winning the German Touring Car Championship with a V8 Quattro in 1991.

By 1995 Biela was behind the wheel of an A4 Quattro in which he won the Touring Car World Cup at the Paul Ricard circuit in Provence. In 1996 the A4 was entered in the British Touring Car Championship, with Frank Biela backed by John Brintcliffe. The four-wheel drive of the Audi conferred such a clear advantage over the rest of the field that a special penalty was imposed on them midway through the season, in that they were forced to carry extra weight. Despite this and undergoing an operation on his back,

Frank Biela still became BTCC champion.

The A4 was also a championship winner in Germany, Spain, Australia, South Africa and Belgium, proving the effectiveness of four-wheel drive on tarmac beyond a shadow of a doubt.

The four Scalextric A4s in the 1998 catalogue were based on Biela's 1996 car, Brad James's 1996 Australian Championship-winning car, Belgian Pro-Car champion Jean-Francis Hemroulle's 1997 winner, and Italian champion Emanuele Pirro's car.

By the middle of the 1997 season, the ballast carried by the Audis in the BTCC series was allowed to be reduced and their performance improved immensely. Not enough, though, for Biela to catch Alain Menu's flying Laguna. Menu took the championship with Biela second, and the Scalextric Laguna for 1998 featured the slightly revised graphics as seen on Menu's 1997 car.

Another newcomer to the 1996 BTCC was the Vectra. John Cleland had been 1995 BTCC winner in the Vauxhall Cavalier, with which he had come second twice and fourth twice since 1990. For 1996, the Vauxhall Sport team replaced the Cavalier with the Vectra, just as the standard production saloon was superseded by the new model. Out on the streets, the Vectra was a major rival to Ford's Mondeo in sales terms, and the rivalry spilled over onto the track. The Vectra couldn't quite keep up

Right Jordan chase McLaren on the cover of 1998's catalogue

with the Audi or the Laguna in its first year, although Cleland's 1996 teammate James Thompson did score one victory with it at Snetterton. The Scalextric Vectras featured John Cleland's 1996 and 1997 Vauxhalls, as well as a car in Opel Motor Sport colours and the Opel-Team Zakspeed car driven by Claus Ludwig in the German championship.

Another saloon racer appearing for the first time in the 1998 catalogue was the Renault Mégane. The Mégane Maxi took over from the Clio Maxi as Renault's front-line rally car. The Maxi cars were what the French termed 'kit cars', highly modified two-wheel-drive machines. In order to take on the four-wheel-drive cars that dominated rallying, manufacturers of two-wheel-drive cars needed to

make massive modifications to boost power, traction and just about everything else. Manufacturing the number of cars required by the FIA rules to qualify the car for competition wasn't really feasible, but manufacturing kits for owners to transform their cars was. Renault was first with the Clio Maxi and others soon followed suit.

The Clio, however, was nowhere near as strong a rally contender as its Mégane sister. The 2-litre Mégane Maxi made its début in the 1996 Rally of Wales and quickly showed an appetite for victory, winning the 1996 Tour de Corse and the Austrian National Rally. In 1998 it won the British and Austrian titles and in 1999 the British and European Championships.

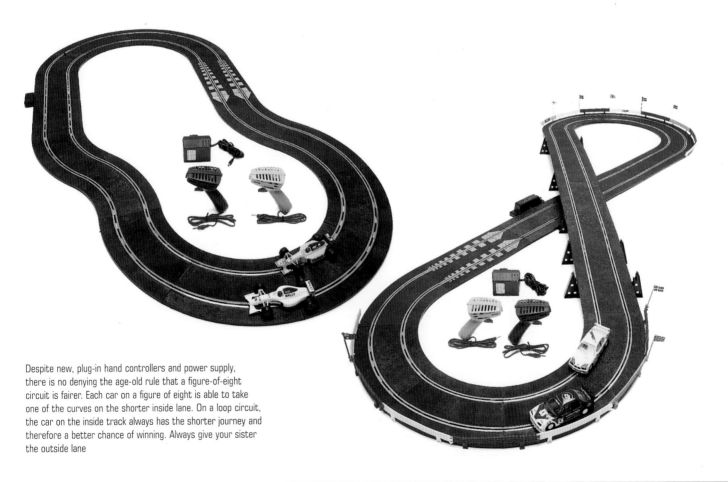

Despite new, plug-in hand controllers and power supply, there is no denying the age-old rule that a figure-of-eight circuit is fairer. Each car on a figure of eight is able to take one of the curves on the shorter inside lane. On a loop circuit, the car on the inside track always has the shorter journey and therefore a better chance of winning. Always give your sister the outside lane

Scalextric's four Méganes were based on the Renault UK cars as driven by Robbie Head and Bryan Thomas in 1996 and 1997, Spanish champion Oriol Gomez's 1997 car, and the Team Diac car in which Philippe Bugalski won the 96 Tour de Corse and came tantalisingly close to winning the French national championship, with second place two years running.

If souped-up saloons weren't to your taste, there was plenty more on Scalextric's 1998 menu to set your mouth watering, including the magnificent Le Mans-winning Porsche 911 GT1. The 3.2 litre turbocharged flat-six Porsches first ran at Le Mans in 1996 where works drivers Hans-Joachim Stuck, Thiery Boutsen and Bob Woolek won their class and came second overall, behind a TWR Porsche, with the Dalmas/Wendlinger/Goodyear car right behind them.

In 97, the 911 GT1 came in fifth and eighth (the TWR Porsche won again), and in 1998 the McNish/Ortiello/Aiello car won, with the Wollek/Muller/Alzen car in second place. Porsche's Le Mans exploits were by now the stuff of legend, but this was still a remarkable result. The two Porsches led home the TWR Nissan with its 3.5-litre turbo power and the 6-litre V12 McLaren F1.

During that same 24 hours in France in 1998, and not all that far from the action at Le Mans, the international distributor of hand tools Teng Tools was holding a sales conference. One of the highlights of the conference was a Scalextric 24-hour race. With four teams of eight drivers, which included four drivers from Scalextric head office and Teng Tools-sponsored Le Mans Porsche driver Stephan Johansson (who won at Le Mans in 1997 and was competing in the Porsche LMP1-98 that year), the race was won by a Porsche 911 GT1. Hardly surprising, really, as all of the competing cars were the same model. Winning twice at Le Mans in the same year is

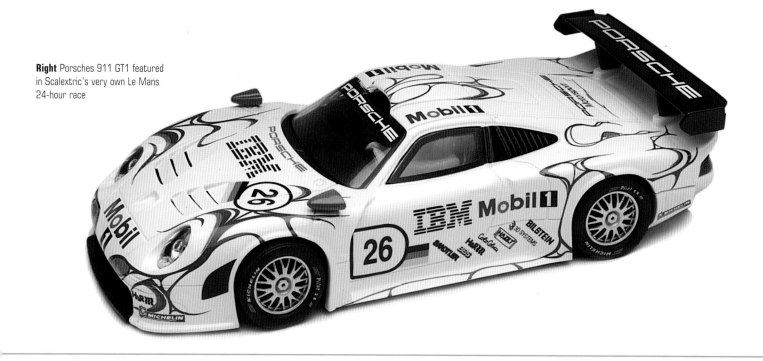

Right Porsches 911 GT1 featured in Scalextric's very own Le Mans 24-hour race

a unique achievement, though, even for Porsche!

The Teng Tools Le Mans featured special Teng Tools-liveried Scalextric cars, but the regular 1998 GT1s that appeared in the catalogue were modelled on the Stuck/Boutsen/Wollek car of 1996 and the Scuderia Italia car raced by Pierluigi Martini and Christian Pescatori in the four-hour races of the 1997 FIA GT championship.

For those who think that saloon car racing is a bit of fun and messing about at Le Mans is like taking a holiday from real motorsport, there is only one game to be in – Formula 1. Scalextric's Formula 1 player for 1998 was the Jordan 197-Peugeot.

Certainly the most eye-catching racing colours on the circuit in 1997, the Jordan's snakeskin decoration gave the car a very aggressive look. Having stepped up from Formula 3000 to Formula 1 in 1991 with the dream of winning within three years, Eddie Jordan was a further four years into reality by the time Giancarlo Fisichella and Ralf Schumacher, whose brother Michael had had a brief flirtation with the Jordan team in 1991, took the Jordan snake out onto the track. The two drivers had a tempestuous relationship but still combined to produce Jordan's best-ever season with both Schumacher and Fisichella making it onto the winners' podium in third place and 'Fisico' taking second in Montreal. Eddie Jordan would have to wait for another year and another driver (Damon Hill) to notch up the team's first Grand Prix win.

A gaggle of Formula 1 cars were given new paint jobs to update them for 1998, and a smattering of single-seat racers were squeezed into the common body style. Demon Tweeks and Valvoline decorated monster trucks rumbled into the arena with Magnatraction to keep them on the straight and narrow, although if they still dared to

misbehave they certainly weren't far beyond the long arm of the law.

There were now no fewer than three cop cars for errant truckers to contend with. The Sierra Cosworth was joined by a Kent Constabulary Vectra and a BMW 320i 'Polizei' car. Quite what one of our

Above Jordan adorned with snakeskin paint scheme

Below Racing Trucks always provided a thrilling spectacle. Watch out for that low bridge, though!

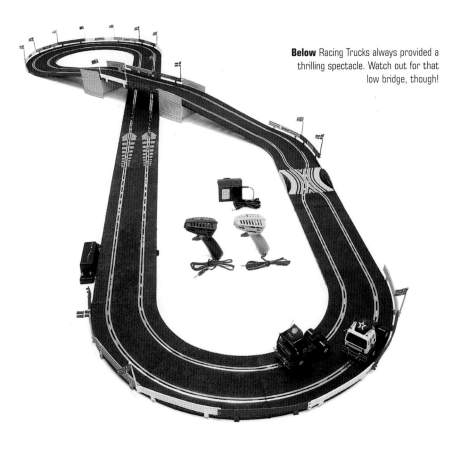

truckers would have made of a German traffic cop takes some imagination:

'Sie fahren viel zu schnell!'

'You wot, mate?'

At last it had arrived. It had been a long wait but some things are worth waiting for. No, not Britain's 'New Labour' government. They'd been around for a couple of years. And no, not Britney Spears, although given the choice between her and Tony Blair . . . No, the big thing everyone was waiting for was the new *Star Wars* movie, *Episode 1 – The Phantom Menace*. Certainly, if Scalextric had had a 'Pod Racing' set it would have blown the Turtles, Spiderman, Batman and Knightrider out of the water.

The Second Millennium's Last Lap

The emphasis at Scalextric in 1999, however, was most definitely on motor sport rather than movie merchandise, and the range featured some

of the most exciting models yet produced.

At the very tip of the motor sport tree, of course, comes Formula 1, so let's start at the top. Making their first catalogue appearances were the Jordan 198-Mugen Honda, the Williams FW20 and the Benetton B193/99. Maybe 1998 was the year Eddie Jordan had been waiting for. Having hired the man he described as 'the world's most expensive guitarist', Damon Hill, to partner Ralf Schumacher, he knew he had real talent behind the wheel. Damon's driving is reputed to be far better than his guitar playing. But would the car work? The new, poised-to-sting hornet nose art gave the Jordan a purposeful look, but in the early part of the season their fiery hornet might just as well have been a floaty butterfly for

Left The Speed 12 with some of its many lights beaming out of the cover of the 1999 catalogue

competing in Formula 3000, and Mugen-Honda had supplied Jordan's F3000 engines. The two Scalextric Jordans for 1999 were numbered 9 and 10 to represent Hill and Schumacher's 1998 cars.

The Williams FW20 appeared not twice but four times in the 1999 catalogue, although two of those appearances were 'under wraps', photographed under a sheet motorshow-style, as the 'new' FW20 (actually the FW21) livery for 1999 was unknown when the catalogue went to press. Or that's the way it seemed at the time. How disappointing, then, that the real-life Alex Zardi and Ralf Schumacher FW21 1999 cars looked so much like the Jacques Villeneuve and Heinz Harald Frentzen FW20 1998 versions. Indeed, the FW20 had only been a mildly redesigned FW19, the car that won Villeneuve the World Championship and brought Williams the driver and constructor championship double for the

all the impact they made. Rapid redesign of the aerodynamics and the settling in of the new Honda engines all came together to produce not only the team's first win but a spectacular 1-2 finish in the Belgian Grand Prix. Damon Hill crossed the line first, closely followed by Schumacher.

For Eddie Jordan it was a dream come true, shared with some old friends. Damon Hill had driven for Jordan when the team was still

Left The Scalextric Jordan for 1999 featured the buzzing hornet graphics of Jordan's 1998 car

second year in a row (the previous year Damon Hill had been Williams's champion). The old red Williams car would, however, soon be superseded by a brand-new dark blue and white model powered by BMW.

Also 'under wraps' in 1999 was the Benetton B199. This also created great false expectation, as the 199 turned out to look almost identical to the 198 in shape, although the graphics differed slightly. It was far from being Benetton's most successful car, with its outdated 'Playfair' Renault V10 engine, and the 1996 Le Mans winner Alexander Wurz could manage only seventh place in the Formula 1 championship, with his teammate Giancarlo Fisichella following him up in ninth.

For endurance race fans there were two new models in 1999: the vigorously styled TVR Speed 12 and the breathtaking Mercedes CLK LM. Designed to race in the same class as

the Porsche 911 GT1, the TVR and Mercedes were superbly detailed. The TVR accurately captured the rounded bodywork of the real car, while the Mercedes had intricate detailing on the engine. Both models had new tyre and wheel combinations, as well as refined Magnatraction for extra grip and a new transverse – sideways – mounted engine. They also had full-length drivers with legs, as opposed to the two-armed crash helmet that drove the Formula 1 cars.

Never short of ideas for new rally cars, for 1999

Right Highly dramatic in its black livery, the Tabac Mercedes was just as impressive on the track as it was in the photographer's studio

Below The Mercedes CLK LM is a stunning model reflecting the powerful styling of the real thing

Above The CLK dominates the 2000 front cover and this plain silver version **(right)** shows how good the model looks from above

Scalextric came up with the Toyota Corolla. The what? Surely the Toyota Corolla is the sort of little runabout that your primary school teacher might use to drive to work? Oh, dear. Did you learn nothing from the Metro 6R4?

The Toyota Corolla works rally car had a 2-litre, 16-valve turbo engine producing around 300

horsepower, and four-wheel drive to get the power down onto the road. It accelerated fast enough to make your primary school teacher wish she'd stayed at home to mark essays, and in the hands of experts like Carlos Sainz and his navigator Luis Moya, it was a worldbeater. The pair won the 1998 Monte Carlo as well as the Rally of New Zealand along with a string of second places spanning the globe from Sweden and Portugal to Argentina and Australia. In 1999 Toyota won the World Rally Championship for manufacturers with the Corolla WRC. The Sainz/Moya car was one of the models available in Scalextric form.

Good as it was, the humble Corolla probably won't be remembered as one of the world's all-time

Above If you can't pronounce Subaru Impreza by now, you either take no interest whatsoever in motorsport or you need a new set of false teeth

Below The Impreza dominated international rallying in the same way that the Audi Quattro had done

Right The Ford Focus bounds out of
the cover of a second edition of the
2000 catalogue

great rally cars. Scalextric's other Japanese
mud-and-gravel merchant most definitely will
go down as an all-time great – the Subaru Impreza.
The Impreza's career in international rallying
began in 1993 when Ari Vatanen took it to second
place in the 1000 Lakes. Subaru didn't have to wait
long for an outright win, though, and the car hasn't
stopped winning since. In 1994 it came first in the
Acropolis with Carlos Sainz piloting, while Colin
McRae won the Rally of New Zealand and the
RAC. An entire mudslide of impressive wins
was followed by 1-2-3 finishes in both the Catalonia
and RAC rallies.

Below There were subtle differences,
mainly around the wheel arches and
in the rear-mounted spare wheel,
between the Caterham and
Lotus 7s in Scalextric form

McRae became the youngest-ever World Rally Champion in 1995 and Subaru took the Manufacturers' trophy. They would win it again in 96 and 97, though the car evolved into a two-door rather than a four-door. version.

While the catalogue shows a model based on McRae's car, he actually left Subaru mid-season in 1998 to race for Ford.

The final new car for 1999 was actually something of an old car, although it had never been available as a Scalextric model before. The Lotus 7 was as old as Scalextric, having been introduced in

1957. The 7 was always manufactured either as a completed car or as a semi-assembled kit ready for the buyer to finish and make roadworthy. This, of course, made it ideal for anyone who wanted to go racing, as you could build a car to suit your engineering skill, driving talent and bank balance. By 1973 Lotus had moved on a long way from their pioneering days in the Fifties, and the manufacturing rights to the 7 were sold to Caterham Cars. Carrying on the tradition of supplying cars in various stages of build, Caterham actively encouraged their buyers/builders to go racing, and the BBC TV

Right Having deserted Subaru for Ford, Colin McRae's Focus appeared as a Scalextric model in 2000

motoring show *Top Gear* even sponsored a one-make Caterham Super 7 Top Gear Challenge for owner/builder/drivers.

The 1999 crop saw its fair share of repainted cars, none more so than the 'Football Specials'. The dramatic Ferrari F40 was draped in the colours of seven top UK soccer teams. You could choose from Arsenal, Chelsea, Liverpool, Newcastle United, Tottenham Hotspur or the 'Old Firm' of Glasgow Celtic or Glasgow Rangers.

And so into the new century, the new millennium. Scalextric certainly stepped boldly into the 21st century, with the company and the range in better shape than it had been for years. There were eleven sets available in the 2000 catalogue, plus four Micro sets and two simplified Micro starter 1:64 sets for smaller kids – My First Scalextric. To garage all of Scalextric's cars now required the use of a multi-storey car park, as 73 models plus 7 Micros were available. These weren't all different models, of course. There were seven 'Football

Specials,' for example. They did include some interesting new additions, though.

The US Powers Back in

Scalextric's American connections had been growing ever stronger through the efforts of Scalextric USA, and the American influence was graphically illustrated in the three NASCAR sets and ten different variations on Ford Taurus and Pontiac Grand Prix models. Actually, the split was nine Taurus to one Grand Prix. This was the first time that Scalextric had made the NASCAR models available officially in the UK, although two Ford and two Chevrolet racers had been launched in the US market to celebrate NASCAR's 50th anniversary as long ago as 1998. There was certainly no shortage of colour on the sponsor-laden Taurus and Pontiac models, reflecting the ultra-bright paint jobs of the real thing. Half a century may be a long time, but no one will ever accuse NASCAR of having grown old and dull. And there's nothing dull about the speeds at which these cars thunder round the banked NASCAR circuits. This is stock-car racing, 'stock' supposedly meaning that the cars are largely production or 'stock' models. It doesn't quite work out that way, though.

The production Ford Taurus Sho (Super High Output) is no slouch, its 3-litre V6 making it the fastest US-built saloon, with a top speed of around 140 mph, but the NASCAR racers will lap their circuits at an average 200 mph. That's fast by anyone's standards.

Another Ford racer for the 2000 Scalextric catalogue was the Focus. Ford's Escort replacement had been launched in 1998, following the 'World Car' principle of the Mondeo and being sold in the US as well as Europe. By 1999 the Focus was the UK's best-selling car, with more than 103,000 leaving the showrooms that year.

The first of Scalextric's two Focus models was based on Colin McRae's works Martini car which, despite some reliability problems, won two of its first four rallies. The other car was modelled on Dubai millionaire rally ace Mohammed Ben Sulayem's car. Eleven times winner of the Middle East Rally Championship and with over 50 international victories, ben Sulayem's Iridium Team Focus, like

EDITION 42 2001   www.scalextric.com

the McRae car, had a transverse engine and a wealth of detail, right down to the pace notes on the navigator's board.

That assiduous attention to detail was carried through to the outlandish Cadillac Le Mans Prototype. If ever a car deserved the nickname 'Batmobile', this was it. Forget the old BMW, this

Above The 2001 catalogue looked suitably space-age with Cadillac's LMP on the cover

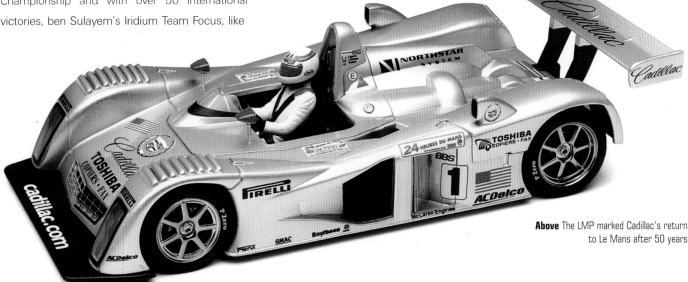

Above The LMP marked Cadillac's return to Le Mans after 50 years

Right The new VW Beetle is a cute car, but it has a mighty racing heart when fitted with the Golf VR6 powerplant

Below Another German V engine, BMW's 3-litre V10 powered the new Williams Formula 1 car

baby really made it feel like a huge disappointment when the driver climbed out and he wasn't wearing a mask, a cape and his pants over his trousers.

The Cadillac LMP, powered by Cadillac's Northstar 4-litre twin turbo V8, was the car that took Cadillac back to Le Mans in 2000, 50 years after a 'Caddie' had last run in the Le Sarthe race. There was a particularly strong American presence at Le Mans that year, with Dodge Vipers and Chevvy Corvettes also competing. The Cadillacs didn't win, but three of the four entered did finish in a race where only 27 of the 48 starters managed to stay the distance. Being there was the important thing. The race was seen by General Motors as part of their overall plan to promote Cadillac around the globe in the run-up to the 100th anniversary of the marque in 2002.

The Beetle – Bigger than Jesus

Another unusual car from Scalextric in 2000 was the 'New' Volkswagen Beetle. Developed from Concept One, a design study carried out by VW's Californian studio, the New Beetle was unveiled at the Detroit Motor Show in 1994. America loved it, doubtless something to do with the fact that 5 million of the original had been sold in the US, and by late 1997 the concept car had become a reality. Although the Mexican-built base model was fairly pedestrian by modern standards, with a top speed of just 110 mph, two of the Scalextric variants were based on the far slicker RSi Beetle, which was powered by the 2.8-litre V6 from the Golf VR6, making it far too quick a bug for most of us to swat. The other two Scalextric Beetles were a little more relaxed and had the distinction of being the only two cars in the catalogue in 'civilian' clothes rather than racing colours. OK, so a couple of the Lotus/Caterham bunch weren't in racing kit either, but at least their drivers were still wearing crash helmets, as opposed to the Beetle crew's baseball caps.

The Subaru Impreza turned up minus racing livery in the 2000 catalogue too, but made up for it by wearing a police uniform. It joined the Vectra and

the Polizei BMW to replace the Cossie cop car and maintain a Scalextric squad-car strength of three.

And that's where the departure, such as it was, from motor sport ends. The only other new models featured for 2000 were members of motor sport's Formula 1 Royal Family. The striking new Williams racing livery on the Williams BMW for 2000 was a blue so deep that it often looked black against the white of the rest of the bodywork. BMW's 3-litre V10 engine proved to be a reliable workhorse, giving drivers Ralf Schumacher and the dazzling new young star Jenson Button the chance to accumulate enough points to ensure a third place in the Constructors' Championship behind McLaren and Ferrari.

The McLaren, in fact, was the other Formula 1 car to take a bow in the 2000 catalogue. Although it had changed little from the previous Scalextric version, the two McLarens now carried the names 'Mika' and 'David' (Hakkinen and Coulthard) on their flanks as part of their revised graphics. Between them the two McLaren drivers had taken their team to second place in the Constructors' Championship two years in succession. The previous year (1998) they had won it. Scalextric's version of Hakkinen's car was modelled on the one in which he became World Champion for the second year in succession. In 2000 he would have to settle for second place behind Ferrari's Michael Schumacher, with teammate Coulthard backing him up in third.

Scalextric powered on into the new century, then, with the same basic philosophy that had carried them forward from 1957 – successful sporting cars are required for what is essentially a car-racing toy. Forget delivery vans, standard saloons, anonymous people carriers, garbage trucks and milk-floats, what you want to see racing round a slotted track is exactly what you would expect to see racing round a real track. Until the whole world abandons the idea of racing motor cars, then, Scalextric will always be there, reflecting reality in miniature as motor sport's twelve-volt baby brother.

Below The McLaren in which Mika Hakkinen became World Champion

Back to Battery Power

Above The new 1990 grandstand could be fitted on top of the new pit-stop

By 1990 motor sport, particularly Formula 1, was more popular than ever before. BTCC events in the Nineties could attract crowds of up to 30,000. To accommodate the swarms of little plastic spectators bustling around your Scalextric circuit, a new grandstand was available which could be located on the roof of the separate pit-stop facility. A stairway at the side allowed the spectators to reach their seats without tripping over the various jacks, trolleys and refuelling aids that were scattered around the pit area, which is just as well because the First Aid Hut building hadn't been available for years.

You weren't likely to want as many as 30,000 tiny plastic people poking their tiny plastic noses in, milling about the track, getting in the way and being trodden on while you were trying to concentrate on a major race. No doubt you would have to let some of them stand and watch, though, and to save you constantly having to make announcements over the Public Address System to stop the spectators walking across the track, there was a brand-new feature for 1990.

The Control Tower and Crosswalk Kit consisted of two towers, one topped with an authentic-looking race control observation gallery, joined by a windowed viewing walkway which could bridge one or two track widths. That would keep the pesky spectators out of harm's way.

Spectators crowding the track would be the last thing you'd want if you'd invested in 1991's new track support piers, and possibly a few extra curves, to create 'an exciting new Scalextric multi-level track support system' which would 'provide a sturdy racing track up to four levels high'. Now why on earth would you want to have a four-tier racing circuit? Well, the idea was that perhaps just part of your circuit would spiral upwards – and presumably downwards again. This was intended to create the effect of racing up a hill or mountain. 'Scalextric vehicles are enthusiastic climbers,' boasted the catalogue, 'and driving over an "Alpine" track is enormous fun.' Ah, there's the word that justifies it all – 'fun'. The catalogue illustration may have looked like a cross between a multi-storey car park and Spaghetti Junction, but it was undoubtedly yet another way to add to the fun of Scalextric racing.

To simulate the really gripping experience of haring up an Alpine road, though, you'd have to make sure that it was pitch-dark, your driver couldn't see round the bend, and there was an articulated truck coming *down* the mountain on the same side of the track. Go on, share my nightmare.

One thing that might make the nightmare's ensuing mountainside carnage less likely was the introduction of the new Permalite system. Its control box allowed you to switch the lights of your Permalite cars on or off whether the cars were moving or stationary. Old-style illuminated cars, whose lights would dim or brighten depending on how fast they were going, could still be used with the system, but with Permalite switched on, you had full beam on all the time. Enough light, in fact, to pick out the whites of that truck-driver's eyes as you rounded the bend on the Alpine track.

Tucked away at the back of the 1991 catalogue were the Ascot and Newmarket horse-racing sets with the new 'Fairweather Lady' dapple grey horse and 'Tim's Folly' chestnut nag . . . sorry . . . thoroughbred. These would soon be joined by the four-horse Derby set and the Gold Coast Cup (based on the famous Australian event) set, which featured two horses pulling 'sulky' trotting buggies. The Derby and Newmarket sets each included two grandstands adapted from the motor-sport range.

Below Battery power saved on electricity and saved your vocal chords as Supersound stepped in to stop you having to do all your own sound effects

The horse-racing sets adhered to the Scalextric prime directive of being fun to use, but they weren't nearly as realistic as the Scalextric cars. How could they be when the model cars ran on wheels, just like the real thing, and the model horses swished round on wheeled trolleys instead of galloping along with their legs a blur? Mind you, you might not want a Scalextric horse-racing set to be too realistic. After all, real horses dump more than just the odd spot of oil on the track.

By 1992, the old sound-effects record would have been impossible to listen to on your CD player, the Twin Auto Screams had been banned by an Act of Parliament (or so my dad told me), and with all of the lights and electrical gadgets attached to your track there probably wasn't enough juice left to power the Sound Track machine. So where were your authentic racing noises supposed to come from, given that going 'Brrrrrrmmmmmmmmmm . . .' for more than a couple of hours would leave you with laryngitis? Why, the new Scalextric Supersound machine, of course. Powered by two AA batteries, the Supersound gave you an engine-revving sound when you held down the 'Revving' button, shifting

to a constant engine tone when you released it, and a changing tone again as you moved up through the gears when you pressed the 'Gear' button. An instant cure for sore throats and an end to the much overrated phenomenon of 'peace and quiet'.

By 1993 the new 'Easi-fit' guide blade incorporating pick-up braids was standard across much of the range. As its name suggests, the Easi-fit simplified the replacement of worn braids. Previously, this was a bit of a fiddly job, not best suited to anyone who was large in the finger department but short on patience. The 1993 catalogue described Easi-fit as making 'the replacement of worn braids a job that can be done in seconds with no fuss or loss of temper'. Obviously somebody on the copywriting team had intimate knowledge of the sort of trackside tantrums that can

Above Details of the Control Tower and Crosswalk that kept pesky spectators off your track

Left The gee-gees were given a whole new lease of life in the Nineties, although they had yet to set hoof on the track

Right The 36 Track Plans booklet – ideal for keeping dad out of the way while also letting him feel he's in charge

turn a rainy Scalextric afternoon into a stuck indoors nightmare from hell. The answer always used to be to calm your dad down and leave him in front of the TV watching an old Gregory Peck movie until you'd sorted out the problem. Nowadays there simply was no problem . . . except that you were stuck with Dad.

Still, why not put him to good use by letting him think that he was in charge? You could give him the new *36 Track Plans* booklet and let him try to plan a layout on which he might actually be able to beat you.

Setting up the new layout became substantially simpler and quicker by 1993 too. Far less valuable racing time needed to be spent on wiring up your transformer and hand controls, for a start. The new Power Base unit connected directly to the track and the transformer was now a wall-plug unit. The lead from the transformer plugged into the Power Base, as did the leads from the new hand controls. There were still a couple of old-fashioned 'screw-down' contacts, but these were for ancillary accessories such as the flashing hazard lights on illuminated chicanes.

Also new for 1993 was another noise-making effort. The Megasound Hand Throttle incorporated the best elements of the Supersound machine within a hand-control unit. It ran on battery power, so it wasn't draining power from your track, but it also responded to your 'driving' actions. You pushed a button on the back of the Megasound controller to give the noise of and engine starting and then ticking over. Then, when you squeezed the throttle trigger, the engine noise raced up through the gear changes to top speed. Lifting off the throttle brought you back to a steady revving sound.

Sadly, Megasound didn't give you a crunching of oats, neighing and galloping hoofs for the horse-

racing sets, but you can't have everything, can you?

Around the mid-Nineties a new range of ready-painted figures was available. There were six spectators, six driver/mechanic models and six pit-crew statues. They weren't exactly young, though. In fact, the little plastic people must have been hard to find at least one day a week, as they would be down the Post Office picking up their pensions. The same figures, described as 'hand painted and unbreakable', had first been seen in Scalextric catalogues 30 years before. Minor modifications, such as the driver who was originally casually holding a cigarette having his habit curtailed, brought the figures up to date, and they would have felt completely at home in among the traffic cones and straw bales that were also being offered in a new pack. They also dated back to the Sixties.

Unpainted seated spectators closely resembling their older relatives who sat in the open grandstand in the Sixties sat in a new version of the old

Right Megasound hand controllers provided yet another opportunity to annoy the neighbours

grandstand in the Nineties. They looked out over a track dotted with new pit-stop and control tower buildings that were also straight out of the Sixties and a new version of the old Dunlop Bridge – now the Goodyear Bridge – to make them feel right at home.

There's nothing wrong with old model buildings being dusted down and put to good use again, of course. If they added to the realism of Scalextric racing in the Sixties, there's no reason why they shouldn't do just as good a job in the Nineties. The buildings were either push-fit assembly with a selection of stickers for decoration or kit-build structures that required the use of the model aircraft and car builder's favourite thing – polystyrene cement. Catch a few too many whiffs of that stuff while you were piecing together your trackside buildings and you just wouldn't be able to resist adding the boldest of psychedelic graffiti when you were painting them. The Goths and Punks you painted among the spectators would love it.

Reintroducing the old designs for buildings and other purely decorative accessories was the best possible way for Scalextric to keep costs down. Creating new items from scratch would have required a great deal of investment which might have proved unviable. That may go some way towards explaining why Micro Scalextric never had the same sort of accessories as its bigger brother. Micro Scalextric did, naturally, have its own lap counter, chicanes, crash barriers and other essentials for competitive racing. It wasn't without a few fun items, either, such as its own daredevil loop, which was available separately as well as part of the G-force Skyloop set. Giant-sized fun from the teensy little cars.

In 1998 a new type of hand control was introduced which did away with the old Flash Gordon ray-gun style, replacing it with a Star Trek phaser style, although it still had a trigger action. The redesigned hand throttle was intended to give more control, and complete control was just what you needed now, because from 1998 onwards you might find yourself competing not only against your opponent but also against the track. The new battery-powered Pole Position Sound Control Centre added another authentic-looking building to your circuit, but the placid exterior hid a truly devious device.

Essentially, it was a lap timer, but this one didn't let you sweep your poorer lap times under the carpet. After setting the machine, it gave you one free warm-up lap before its timer kicked in the next time you crossed the start line. It would then record your 'qualifying time', and when you next crossed the start line the machine actually announced your lap time for all to hear. It could also be set to show flashing lights and sound a horn for the start of a race, whereupon it would supply engine noises and give a lap count-down to the end of the race. For its last trick it announced the winner as the car crossed the finishing line and supplied cheers from the crowd. About the only thing it didn't do was pop open a bottle of champagne and spray it in the air.

A certain amount of silliness such as this was required to offset the appearance of some serious racing equipment. Just as the Race Tuned cars had done in the past, 1999's Protec models gave the dedicated competitor something to get his teeth into, although a screwdriver would have been more useful. Protec cars, launched with the Vectra and Audi A4, came broken down into kit form, allowing you to customise your car to suit your racing style and the circuit on which you were about to race.

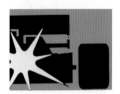
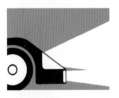

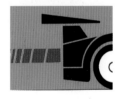

Above Nineties catalogues were awash with symbols representing special features on cars such as Magnatraction, Permalite, Turboflash and CD multi-changer. No, not CD multi-changer but Scalextric cars now had almost as many options as the real thing

Above The Pole Position Sound Control Centre left you nowhere to hide – it announced your lap times for all to hear

Assembly required no glue or painting and the minimum of tools. Teeth were not an essential requirement. The components were assembled and fitted to a two-piece metal chassis. You could adjust the positioning of the Magnatraction magnets to best suit the car you were racing, and choose from three different gear ratios for optimum performance. Finally, you attached the bodywork and you were ready to race. At a special Protec Challenge event on the 100 foot track at Newcastle's Riverside Raceway slot-car venue, one of the 12 teams managed to get their car going in just 35 minutes. Only two teams failed to have their cars ready to race within the one-hour time limit. One team did, however, set off on their practice lap in reverse, having obviously managed to assemble something the wrong way round. Serious racing always has its lighter moments.

Major innovations for the start of the 21st century included three new electronic gizmos.

The Power Plus system was a more elaborate form of the Power Base, allowing separate power supply from separate transformers to each lane of

your track. This meant that your car was always operating with the maximum available power input for maximum potential performance. To help take the edge off your speed for tricky corners or chicanes, the system also had a special braking facility. With the switch in the 'brakes on' position, it slowed your car dramatically when you released the throttle. Like the Power Base, Power Plus gave you the option of racing on your circuit in the opposite direction without having to mess around re-fitting the power supply. All you had to do was flick a switch. You had to remember to turn your cars around, of course, unless you wanted to 'stage a reversing contest.

The new century provided the perfect excuse, if ever one had been needed, to introduce yet another form of lap counter. The new electronic counter was a 'black box' like the other new systems, rather than being disguised as a trackside structure, and would count down a race from up to 99 laps. It also gave the fastest lap time for each lane on a digital display, emitting an attention-grabbing sound when a new fastest lap was achieved and when each lap was completed.

Rounding off the black box line-up was the Pacer system. This could also be used in place of the standard Power Base and gave you the option of racing against a ghost partner. The machine would record the way you drove your 'best lap' and then faultlessly repeat it, driving a car around the circuit on automatic pilot. This gave you an opponent to race against even if you were the smelliest, most antisocial nerd in the universe and had no friends to play with. Should someone take pity on you and agree to a race, the Pacer could

Below Three new 'black box' electronic gizmos in 2000 gave you even more control over your Scalextric racing but they still couldn't keep the dratted car on the track!

revert to manual control of both lanes. It also provided a flashing light sequence to start a race, ensuring that you didn't immediately lose your new-found friend by shouting 'Go!' just that little bit *after* you set off . . .

If all of that 21st-century technology still left you hungering for the sort of computer-aided race management so essential for Formula 1 teams, then the Interactive Race Control system (or Race Management System) was what you had been waiting for. Now you could programme an entire race into your computer and monitor the progress of each car on screen to check the details of its last lap, fastest lap, number of laps completed and other essential information on the constantly updated central scoreboard. Other features included an animation of a pit-stop initiated by low fuel or the request of a racer.

Storing the final race results – drivers, cars and times – on computer also meant that you could instantly refute claims such as, 'I beat you easily two weeks ago when you were driving a McLaren and all I had was a manky old Austin Maestro.'

You could also use the Race Control CD to design track layouts and even access the Scalextric web site for all of the latest info on new product releases.

All of that was for the dedicated Scalextric fan, or for club racers who could make best use of the system. At the other end of the technological scale, Scalextric drivers were being recruited at an ever younger age.

My First Scalextric was a simplified version of Micro Scalextric. Two sets were initially offered aimed at racers as young as three. The cars were Formula 1 style racers or Jaguar XJ220 models, with as few parts as possible that could be snapped off and eaten. Keeping your future clients fit and healthy is obviously a major priority!

With the range more diverse than it had been since the glorious boom years of the Sixties, and sophisticated new product lines keeping the toy that had been around for almost half a century bang up to date, Scalextric looked firmly set to keep on racing well past its 50th birthday. What next, though? Cars where you can change gear just like the real thing? Drivers that cost you a king's ransom just like the real thing? Virtual-reality Scalextric racing helmets?

Let's face it, most of us would settle for cars that simply put themselves back on the track. On the other hand, that's all part of the fun, isn't it? And almost fifty years on from the first Scalextric race, fun is still what it's all about.

Above New hand throttles designed to give extra control

Left My First Scalextric is aimed at younger kids to get 'em hooked on Scalextric before they're old enough to say 'Gameboy'. . .

Left . . . and the Interactive Race Control System will keep 'em hooked even after they turn into teenage computer geeks, thus ensuring the survival of Scalextric well into the new Millennium

UK Catalogue Cars

1960
MM/C.54 Lotus
MM/C.55 Vanwall
MM/C.56 Lister Jaguar
MM/C.57 Aston Martin

1961
MM/C.54 Lotus
MM/C.55 Vanwall
MM/C.56 Lister Jaguar
MM/C.57 Aston-Martin
MM/C.58 Cooper
MM/C.59 BRM
MM/C.60 D-type Jaguar
MM/C.61 Porsche

1962
MM/C.54 Lotus
MM/C.55 Vanwall
MM/C.56 Lister Jaguar
MM/C.57 Aston Martin
MM/C.58 Cooper
MM/C.59 BRM
MM/C.60 D-type Jaguar
MM/C.61 Porsche
MM/C.62 Ferrari
MM/C.63 Lotus
MM/C.64 Bentley
MM/C.65 Alfa Romeo

1963
C.54 Lotus
C.55 Vanwall
C.56 Lister Jaguar
C.57 Aston Martin
C.58 Cooper
C.59 BRM

C.60 D-type Jaguar
C.61 Porsche
C.62 Ferrari
C.63 Lotus
C.64 Bentley
C.65 Alfa Romeo
C.66 Cooper
C.67 Lotus
C.68 Aston Martin
C.69 Ferrari
C.70 Bugatti
C.71 Auto Union
B/1 Typhoon
B/2 Hurricane

1964
C.54 Lotus
C.55 Vanwall
C.58 Cooper
C.60 D-type Jaguar
C.61 Porsche
C.62 Ferrari
C.64 Bentley
C.65 Alfa Romeo
C.66 Cooper
C.67 Lotus
C.68 Aston Martin
C.69 Ferrari
C.70 Bugatti
C.71 Auto-Union
C.72 BRM
C.73 Porsche
C.74 Austin Healey 3000
C.75 Mercedes 190SL
B/1 Typhoon
B/2 Hurricane
E5 Marshal's Car

1965
C.54 Lotus
C.55 Vanwall
C.58 Cooper
C.60 D-type Jaguar
C.61 Porsche
C.62 Ferrari
C.64 Bentley
C.65 Alfa Romeo
C.66 Cooper
C.67 Lotus
C.68 Aston Martin
C.69 Ferrari GT
C.70 Bugatti
C.71 Auto-Union
C.72 BRM
C.73 Porsche
C.74 Austin Healey 3000
C.75 Mercedes 190SL
C.76 Mini Cooper
B/1 Typhoon
B/2 Hurricane
K1 Go-Kart
E5 Marshal's car

1966
C.54 Lotus
C.64 Bentley
C.65 Alfa Romeo
C.68 Aston Martin
C.69 Ferrari GT
C.74 Austin Healey 3000
C.75 Mercedes 190 SL
C.76 Mini Cooper
C.77 Ford
C.78 AC Cobra
C.79 Offenhauser Front Engine

C.80 Offenhauser Rear Engine
C.81 Cooper
C.82 Lotus
C.83 Sunbeam Tiger
C.84 Triumph TR4A
C.85 BRM
C.86 Porsche
C.87 Vanwall Race Tuned
C.88 Cooper Race Tuned
C.89 BRM Race Tuned
C.90 Ferrari Race Tuned
C.91 D-type Jaguar Race Tuned
C.92 Porsche Race Tuned
C.93 Austin Healey 3000 Race
    Tuned
C.94 Mercedes 190 SL Race
    Tuned
C.95 Bugatti Race Tuned
C.96 Auto-Union Race Tuned
B/1 Typhoon
B/2 Hurricane
K1 Go-Kart
E5 Marshal's car

1967
C.54 Lotus
C.64 Bentley
C.65 Alfa Romeo
C.68 Aston Martin
C.69 Ferrari GT
C.74 Austin Healey 3000
C.75 Mercedes 190SL
C.76 Mini Cooper
C.77 Ford
C.78 AC Cobra
C.79 Offenhauser Front Engine
C.80 Offenhauser Rear Engine
C.81 Cooper
C.82 Lotus
C.83 Sunbeam Tiger
C.84 Triumph TR4A
C.85 BRM
C.86 Porsche
C.87 Vanwall Race Tuned
C.88 Cooper Race Tuned
C.89 BRM Race Tuned
C.90 Ferrari Race Tuned
C.91 D-type Jaguar Race Tuned

Below D-type Jaguars

C.92 Porsche Race Tuned

C.93 Austin Healey 3000 Race Tuned

C.94 Mercedes 190 SL Race Tuned

C.95 Bugatti Race Tuned

C.96 Auto-Union Race Tuned

K.1 Go-Kart

B/1 Typhoon Combination

B/2 Hurricane Combination

1968

C.1 Alpine Renault

C.2 Matra Jet

C.3 Javelin Special

C.4 Electra Special

C.5 Europa Vee

C.6 Panther

C.7 Rally Mini Cooper

C.10 Super Javelin Race Tuned

C.11 Super Electra Race Tuned

C.32 Mercedes 250SL

C.54 Lotus

C.60 D-type Jaguar

C.61 Porsche

C.64 Bentley

C.65 Alfa Romeo

C.68 Aston Martin

C.69 Ferrari GT

C.74 Austin Healey 3000

C.75 Mercedes 190SL

C.77 Ford GT

C.78 A C Cobra

C.79 Offenhauser Front Engine

C.80 Offenhauser Rear Engine

C.83 Sunbeam Tiger

C.84 Triumph TR4

C.88 Cooper Race Tuned

C.89 BRM Race Tuned

C.90 Ferrari Race Tuned

C.93 Austin Healey Race Tuned

C.94 Mercedes 190SL Race Tuned

C.95 Bugatti Race Tuned

C.96 Auto-Union

C.99 Fiat 600

B/1 Typhoon

B/2 Hurricane

1969

C.1 Alpine Renault

C.2 Matra Jet

C.3 Javelin

C.4 Electra

C.5 Europa Vee

C.6 Panther

C.7 Mini Cooper rooflight

C.8 Lotus Indianapolis

C.9 Ferrari

C.14 Matra GP

C.15 Ford Mirage

C.16 Ferrari P4

C.17 Lamborghini

C.18 Ford 3L GT

C.19 Scalextric Team Car

C.32 Mercedes 250SL

C.36 Honda GP

C.77 Ford GT

C.79 Offenhauser Front Engine

C.80 Offenhauser Rear Engine

C.83 Sunbeam Tiger

C.84 Triumph TR 4A

C.99 Fiat 600

B/1 Typhoon

B/2 Hurricane

1970

C.3 Javelin

C.4 Electra

C.5 Europa Vee

C.6 Panther

C.7 Mini Cooper roof light

C.8 Lotus Indianapolis

C.9 Ferrari

C.14 Matra GP

C.15 Ford Mirage

C.16 Ferrari P4

C.17 Lamborghini

C.18 Ford 3L GT

C.19 Scalextric Team Car

C.20 Dart GP

C.21 Cougar Sports

C.32 Mercedes 250 SL

C.36 Honda GP

C.77 Ford GT

C.79 Offenhauser Front Engine

C.83 Sunbeam Tiger

Above Aston Martin DBR

C.84 Triumph TR4A

C.99 Fiat 600

B/1 Typhoon

B/2 Hurricane

1971

C.3 Javelin Sports

C.4 Electra Sports

C.5 Europa Vee

C.6 Panther GP

C.7 Mini Cooper

C.8 Lotus Indianapolis

C.9 Ferrari

C.14 Matra GP

C.15 Ford Mirage

C.16 Ferrari P4

C.17 Lamborghini

C.18 Ford 3L GT

C.19 Scalextric Team Car

C.21 Cougar Sports

C.22 Porsche 917 GT

C.23 Scaletti-Arrow

C.24 Team Car Mk.II

C.32 Mercedes 250SL

C.34 E-type Jaguar

C.36 Honda GP

C.37 BRM

C.65 Alfa Romeo

C.83 Sunbeam Tiger

C.84 Triumph TR4A

C.96 Auto Union

1972

C.3 Javelin

C.4 Electra

C.7 Mini Cooper

C.8A Lotus Indianapolis

C.9 Ferrari

C.14A Matra

C.15 Ford Mirage

C.16 Ferrari P4

C.17 Lamborghini

C.18 Ford 3L

C.21 Cougar

C.22 Porsche 917

C.23 Scalletti Arrow

C.24A Mark II Team Car

C.26 March Ford 721

C.32 Mercedes 250SL

C.34 E-type Jaguar

C.37A BRM

C.41 Ferrari GT 330

C.44 Mercedes Wankel C.111

1973

C.3 Javelin

C.4 Electra

C.7 Mini

C.15 Ford Mirage

C.16 Ferrari P4

C.17 Lamborghini

C.22 Porsche 917

C.23 Scalletti Arrow

C.25 Ferrari 312B2

C.26 March Ford 721

C.28 Renault Alpine

C.37 BRM

C.41 Ferrari 330GT

C.43 McLaren M9A

C.44 Mercedes Wankel C111

C.46 Porsche 917K

C.47 Tyrrell Ford

C.50 JPS Lotus 72

1974

C.7 Mini
C.12 Shadow
C.13 Tiger Special Sports
C.15 Ford Mirage
C.16 Ferrari P4
C.17 Lamborghini
C.23 Scalletti Arrow
C.25 Ferrari 312B2
C.26 March Ford 721
C.48 Tyrrell Ford
C.50 JPS Lotus 72
C.52 Escort Mexico

1975

C.7 Mini
C.12 Shadow
C.23 Scalletti Arrow
C.25 Ferrari 312B2
C.26 March Ford 721
C.50 JPS Formula 1
C.51 BRM P160
C.52 Escort Mexico
C.53 Datsun 260Z

1976

C.26 March Ford 721
C.50 JPS Lotus 72
C.51 BRM P160
C.52 Escort Mexico
C.53 Datsun 260Z
C.120 Martini Brabham BT44B

C.121 Elf Tyrrell
C.122 Mini Clubman
C.123 UOP Shadow
C.124 Ferrari 312 T

1977

C.26 March Ford 721
C.51 BRM P160
C.52 Escort Mexico
C.53 Datsun 260Z
C.120 Martini Brabham BT44B
C.121 Elf Tyrrell 007
C.122 Mini Clubman
C.123 UOP Shadow
C.124 Ferrari 312 T
C.125 Porsche Turbo 935
C.126 JPS Lotus 77
C.127 Marlboro McClaren M23

1978

C.51 BRM P160
C.52 Escort
C.120 Brabham BT44B
C.121 Elf Tyrrell 007
C.122 Mini Clubman
C.123 Shadow UOP
C.124 Ferrari 312 T
C.125 Porsche 935 Turbo
C.126 JPS Lotus 77
C.127 Marlboro McClaren M23
C.128 BMW Turbo 320
C.129 6 Wheel March Ford 240
C.130 Triumph TR7

1979

C.51 BRM P160
C.52 Escort Mexico
C.120 Brabham BT44B
C.122 Mini Clubman
C.123 Shadow UOP
C.125 Porsche 935 Turbo
C.126 Lotus 77
C.127 McClaren M23
C.128 BMW 3.0 CSL
C.129 6 Wheel March Ford
C.130 Triumph TR7
C.133 Wolf WR5
C.134 Renault RS-01
C.135 Tyrrell 008
C.136 Ferrari 312 T3

1980

C.103 BRM P160
C.104 Brabham BT44B
C.105 Shadow UOP
C.106 Wolf WR5 blue
C.107 Wolf WR5 red
C.108 McClaren M23
C.109 Escort Mexico
C.110 Mini Clubman white
C.112 Mini Clubman green
C.113 Triumph TR7 red
C.114 Triumph TR7 yellow
C.115 Porsche 935
C.116 BMW 3.0 CSL
C.117 Ford Capri
C.118 Escort with lights
C.119 Porsche with lights
C.126 Lotus 77
C.131 March Ford 771
C.134 Elf Renault RS-01
C.135 Elf Tyrrell 008
C.136 Ferrari 312 T3
C.137 Ligier JS11
C.281 Motorcycle sidecar red
C.282 Motorcycle sidecar green

1981

C.103 BRM P160

Left Mini 1275 GTs

1979

C.104 Brabham BT 44B
C.105 Shadow U.O.P
C.106 Wolf WR5 blue
C.107 Wolf WR5 red
C.108 McClaren M23
C.109 Escort Mexico
C.110 Mini Clubman white
C.112 Mini Clubman green
C.113 Triumph TR7 red
C.114 Triumph TR7 yellow
C.115 Porsche Turbo 935
C.116 BMW 3.0 CSL
C.117 3.0 Ford Capri
C.126 Lotus 77
C.131 March Ford 771
C.134 Elf Renault RS-01
C.135 Elf Tyrrell 008
C.136 Ferrari 312 T3
C.137 Ligier JS 11
C.281 Motorcycle sidecar red
C.282 Motorcycle sidecar green
C.283 Rover 3500
C.284 Police Rover
C.287 Escort with lights
C.288 Porsche silver with lights
C.289 Porsche gold with lights

1982

C.104 Brabham
C.105 Shadow UOP
C.106 Wolf WR5 blue
C.109 Escort
C.110 Rally Mini Clubman white
C.112 Rally Mini Clubman green
C.113 Triumph TR7 red
C.114 Triumph TR7 yellow
C.115 Porsche 935 Turbo
C.116 BMW 3.0 CSL
C.117 Ford Capri
C.126 Lotus 77
C.131 March Ford 771
C.134 Elf Renault Turbo RS-01
C.135 Elf Tyrrell 008
C.136 Ferrari 312 T3
C.137 Ligier JS11
C.138 Saudi Leyland Williams
C.139 Brabham BT49
C.280 PMG Rover

C.281 Motorcycle sidecar red
C.282 Motorcycle sidecar green
C.283 Triplex Rover
C.284 Police Rover
C.287 Escort
C.288 Porsche silver
C.289 Porsche gold
C.294 Triumph TR7
C.295 Porsche Turbo
C.296 BMW 3.0 CSL
C.300 Ford Capri 3.0
C.303 Datapost Metro
C.304 McCain Metro
C.305 Bentley
C.306 Alfa Romeo

1983

C.137 Ligier JS11
C.138 Saudia Leyland Williams
C.139 Brabham BT49c
C.280 PMG Rover
C.283 Triplex Rover
C.290 Banger Racer red
C.291 Banger Racer blue
C.303 Datapost Metro
C.304 McCain Metro
C.305 Bentley
C.306 Alfa Romeo
C.307 XR3 red
C.308 XR3 silver
C.309 TR7
C.311 Capri
C.288 Porsche Turbo silver
C.289 Porsche Turbo gold
C.311 Capri Lights/Spoiler
C.312 Stox Car silver
C.313 Stox Car gold

1984

C.137 Ligier JS11
C.138 Saudia Leyland Williams
C.139 Brabham BT49c
C.288 Porsche Turbo silver
C.289 Porsche Turbo gold
C.311 Capri
C.315 Police car
C.330 Golden Wonder Rover
C.331 Melitta Metro

C.332 MG Maestro
C.333 XR4i blue
C.334 XR4i yellow
C.340 Marshal's car
C.341 XR3i red
C.342 XR3i silver
C.347 BMW M1
C.348 Audi Quattro
C.350 Casio Formula 2 Car
C.351 Grand Prix International
      Formula 3 Car

1985

C.137 Ligier JS11
C.138 Saudia Leyland Williams
C.139 Brabham BT49c
C.288 Porsche Turbo silver
C.289 Porsche Turbo gold
C.311 Capri
C.330 Golden Wonder Rover
C.331 Melitta Metro
C.332 MG Maestro
C.333 XR4i blue
C.334 XR4i yellow
C.340 Marshal's car
C.341 XR3i red
C.342 XR3i silver
C.347 BMW M1
C.348 Audi Quattro
C.350 Casio Formula 2 Car
C.351 Grand Prix International
      Formula 3 Car
C.360 6R4 Metro Ternco
C.362 Police car
C.366 1985 Duckhams Metro

1986

C.138 Saudia Leyland Williams
      FWO 7B
C.139 Parmalat Brabham BT49
C.144 Martini Lancia
C.145 Pioneer Lancia
C.149 Computervision Metro 6R4
C.324 Valvoline Metro
C.341 Ford XR3i red
C.342 Ford XR3i silver
C.347 BMW M1
C.348 Audi Quattro

C.356 Track Ace
C.357 Track Burner
C.362 Police car
C.363 Porsche red
C.364 Porsche black
C.366 Duckhams Metro
C.375 Palmer Tube Mills XR3i
C.376 Mobil XR3i
C.377 Tyler Autos Formula 2
C.378 Graves Engineering Formula 2
C.379 Ford Capri 3.0s
C.380 Bison Computers Datsun
      260Z

1987

C.016 Lancia LC2 SRS
C.017 Peugeot 205 Turbo 16 SRS
C.018 Porsche 956 SRS
C.019 Mercedes 190E 2.3-16 SRS
C.138 Saudia Leyland Williams
      FW07B
C.139 Parmalat Brabham BT49
C.144 Team Lancia
C.145 Pioneer Lancia
C.150 Metro 6R4 – withdrawn
C.347 BMW M1
C.349 Audi Quattro
C.362 Police car
C.363 Porsche red
C.364 Porsche black
C.373 Lotus Renault 98T
C.374 Williams Honda FW11
C.375 Palmer Tube Mills XR3i
C.376 Mobil XR3i
C.377 Tyler Autos Formula 2
C.378 Graves Engineering Formula 2
C.379 Rally Capri Special
C.380 Bison Computers Datsun
      260Z
C.383 Pontiac
C.384 Taurus Rover 3500
C.385 Deserra Sports
C.386 Stone Avionics
C.389 Ilford Photos XR3i
C.390 Bosch XR3i
C.391 Ferrari GTO

1988

C.016 Lancia LC2 SRS
C.017 Peugeot 205 Turbo SRS
C.019 Mercedes 190E 2.3-16 SRS
C.020 McClaren F1 SRS
C.021 Ferrari F1 SRS
C.022 Porsche 956 SRS
C.138 Saudia Leyland Williams
      FW07B
C.139 Parmalat Brabham BT49
C.144 Team Lancia
C.145 Pioneer Lancia
C.347 BMW M1
C.349 Audi Quattro
C.362 Police car
C.376 Mobil XR3i
C.379 Rally Capri Special
C.382 Jaguar XJ8
C.384 Taurus Rover 3500
C.389 Ilford Photo XR3i
C.391 Ferrari GTO
C.425 Lotus Renault 98T
C.426 Williams Honda FW11
C.427 Porsche red
C.428 Porsche black
C.433 Pirelli XR3I
C.434 Lotus Honda Turbo
C.436 Porsche 963

1989

C.016 Lancia LC2 SRS
C.017 Peugeot 205 Turbo 16 SRS
C.019 Mercedes 190E 2.3-16 SRS
C.020 McLaren F1 MP4/2B SRS
C.021 Ferrari F1 156/85 SRS
C.022 Porsche 956 SRS
C.138 Saudia Leyland Williams
      FW07B
C.139 Parmalat BT 49
C.144 Team Lancia
C.228 Qudos
C.229 Kötzting
C.347 BMW M1
C.349 Audi Quattro
C.362 Police car
C.376 Mobil XR3i
C.377 Tyler Autos Formula 2
C.378 Graves Engineering Formula 2

C.379 Rally Capri Special
C.380 Bison Computers Datsun 260Z
C.382 Jaguar XJ8
C.384 Taurus Rover 3500
C.385 Deserra Sports
C.386 Stone Avionics
C.391 Ferrari GTO
C.425 Lotus Renault 98T
C.426 Williams Honda FW11
C.427 Porsche red
C.428 Porsche black
C.429 Ford RS200 Radiopaging
C.432 Ford RS200 Shell
C.433 Pirelli XR3i
C.434 Lotus Honda Turbo
C.436 Porsche 962
C.449 Porsche 959
C.455 Cosworth Texaco
C.456 Ford Cosworth
C.457 Ferrari F1

1990
C.144 Team Lancia
C.228 Qudos
C.229 Kötzting
C.238 Motorbike red
C.239 Motorbike yellow flash
C.347 BMW M1
C.362 Police car
C.377 Tyler Autos F2
C.378 Graves Engineering F2
C.379 Rally Capri
C.382 Jaguar XJR9
C.385 Deserra Sports
C.386 Stone Avionics
C.391 Ferrari GTO
C.425 Lotus Renault 98T
C.426 Williams Honda FW11
C.427 Porsche red
C.428 Porsche black
C.429 Ford RS200 Radiopaging
C.432 Ford RS200 Shell
C.434 Lotus Honda Turbo
C.436 Porsche 962
C.449 Porsche 959
C.455 Ford RS Cosworth Texaco
C.456 Ford RS Cosworth Firestone

C.457 Ferrari F1
C.458 Rally Audi Quattro
C.459 Shell Datsun 260Z
C.460 STP XR3i
C.461 Ford Benetton B189
C.462 Honda McLaren MP 4/4
C.463 Shell Porsche 962
C.464 BMW M3
C.467 Tyrrell 018
C.468 Sauber Mercedes C9/88

1991
C.123 Janspeed Ford RS Cosworth
C.124 Fina Porsche 962
C.124 Havoline Porsche 911
C.126 Bardahl Ford XR3i
C.228 Qudos
C.229 Kötzting
C.232 Penzoil Indy
C.233 Toshiba Indy
C.238 'Racing Red' motorbike
C.239 'Yellow Flash' motorbike
C.362 Police car
C.377 Tyler Autos F2
C.378 Graves Engineering F2
C.379 Capri Special
C.382 Jaguar XJR9
C.385 Deserra Sports
C.386 Stone Avionics
C.391 Ferrari GTO
C.405 BMW M1
C.406 BMW M3 Mobil
C.407 Porsche 911
C.408 Ford RS Cosworth Syntronix
C.409 BMW M3 Demon Tweeks
C.411 Lamborghini Diablo
C.418 Purple Jaguar XJR9
C.426 Williams Honda FW11
C.427 Porsche red
C.428 Porsche black
C.429 Ford RS200 Radiopaging
C.432 Ford RS200 Shell
C.434 Lotus Honda Turbo
C.436 Porsche 962
C.449 Porsche 959
C.455 Ford RS Cosworth Texaco
C.457 Ferrari F1
C.458 Audi Quattro

C.459 Shell Datsun 260Z
C.460 STP Escort XR3i
C.461 Ford Benetton B189
C.463 Shell Porsche 962
C.464 BMW M3
C.467 Ford Tyrrell
C.468 Sauber Mercedes C9/88
C.486 Porsche 962 Kenwood

1992
C.102 Team Talbot
C.123 Janspeed Cosworth
C.124 Havoline Porsche
C.126 Bardahl XR3i
C.125 Fina Porsche 962
C.127 Lamborghini Diablo
C.169 Ford RS Cosworth Monroe
C.175 Ford RS Cosworth Cortez
C.188 Take Fuji Porsche
C.189 Sauber Mercedes C9/88
C.228 Qudos
C.229 Kötzting
C.232 Penzoil Indy
C.233 Toshiba Indy
C.238 'Racing Red' motorbike
C.239 'Yellow Flash' motorbike
C.272 'From A' Porsche 962
C.296 Porsche 962C R
C.310 Ferrari F40
C.319 Ferrari 643
C.321 Ford XR2i
C.347 BMW M1
C.362 Police car
C.377 Tyler Autos F2
C.378 Graves Engineering
C.379 Rallye Capri Special
C.382 Castrol Jaguar XJR9
C.385 Dessera Sports
C.386 Stone Avionics
C.391 Ferrari GTO
C.405 BMW M1 silver
C.406 BMW M3 Mobil
C.407 Porsche 911 white
C.408 Ford RS Cosworth Syntron-X
C.409 BMW M3 Demon Tweeks
C.411 Lamborghini Diablo red
C.418 Jaguar XJR9
C.426 Williams Honda FW11

C.427 Porsche 911 red
C.428 Porsche 911 black
C.429 Ford RS200 Radiopaging
C.432 Ford RS200 Shell
C.434 Lotus Honda Turbo
C.436 Autoglass Porsche 962
C.441 Ford Texaco XR3i
C.449 Porsche 959
C.455 Ford RS Cosworth Texaco
C.456 Ford RS Cosworth Firestone
C.457 Ferrari F1
C.458 Audi Quattro
C.459 Shell Datsun
C.460 STP Escort XR3i
C.461 Ford Benetton B189
C.463 Shell Porsche
C.464 BMW M3 black
C.467 Ford Tyrrell 018
C.468 Sauber Mercedes C9/88
C.472 Dunlop F1
C.473 Panasonic F1
C.486 Kenwood Porsche 962

1993
C.123 Ford RS Cosworth Janspeed
C.124 Porsche 911 Havoline
C.125 Porsche 962C Fina
C.127 Lamborghini Diablo
C.150 Mini Cooper
C.169 Ford RS Cosworth Monroe
C.175 Ford RS Cosworth Cortez
C.184 Minardi F1
C.188 Porsche 962C Take Fuji
C.189 Sauber Mercedes C9/88
C.195 Ferrari F40
C.203 Ford Escort Cosworth
C.204 Ford Escort Cosworth Panasonic
C.228 Qudos
C.229 Kötzting
C.238 'Racing Red' motorbike
C.239 'Yellow Flash' motorbike
C.256 'Repsol' Porsche 962C
C.257 Jaguar XJ220
C.272 'From A' Porsche 962C
C.280 Ford RS Cosworth Duckhams
C.296 Porsche 962C R

C.310 Ferrari F40
C.316 Ford XR2i Valvoline
C.319 Ferrari 643
C.321 Ford XR2i
C.350 Gold Star F1
C.351 Exchange Services F1
C.352 Watts Racing F1
C.362 Police car
C.377 Tyler Autos
C.379 Rallye Capri Special
C.382 Castrol Jaguar XJR9
C.385 Deserra Sports
C.386 Stone Avionics
C.391 Ferrari GTO
C.406 BMW M3 Mobil
C.407 Porsche 911
C.408 Ford RS Cosworth Syntron-X
C.409 BMW M3 Demon Tweeks
C.411 Lamborghini Diablo
C.418 Jaguar XJR9
C.423 Ford RS Cosworth Fina
C.426 Williams Honda FW11
C.427 Porsche 911 red
C.428 Porsche 911 black
C.433 Jaguar XJR9
C.436 Autolass Porsche 962C
C.444 Porsche 962C
C.455 Ford RS Cosworth
C.456 Ford RS Cosworth Firestone
C.458 Audi Quattro
C.459 Shell Datsun 260Z
C.460 STP Escort XR3i
C.461 Ford Benetton B189
C.463 Shell Porsche 962C
C.464 BMW M3
C.467 Ford Tyrrell 018
C.486 Kenwood Porsche 962C

1994

C.123 Ford RS Cosworth Janspeed
C.124 Havoline Porsche 911
C.125 Fina Porsche 962C
C.127 Lamborghini Diablo Yellow
C.142 Ford Benetton B193
C.143 Williams Renault FW15C
C.150 Mini Cooper
C.175 Ford RS Cosworth Cortez
C.184 Minardi F92/1

C.189 Sauber Mercedes C9/88
C.195 Ferrari F40 dark blue
C.203 Ford Escort Cosworth
C.204 Ford Escort Cosworth
  Panasonic
C.228 Qudos
C.229 Kötzting Systems
C.238 'Racing Red' motorbike and
  sidecar
C.239 'Yellow Flash' motorbike and
  sidecar
C.256 Repsol Porsche 962C
C.257 Jaguar XJ220
C.272 From A Porsche 962
C.280 Ford RS Cosworth
  Duckhams
C.310 Ferrari F40
C.311 Texaco 500
C.316 Ford Fiesta XR2i Valvoline
C.319 Ferrari 643
C.321 Ford Fiesta XR2I
C.350 Goldstar F1
C.351 Exchange Services F1
C.352 Watts Racing F1
C.379 Rally Capri Special
C.382 'Castrol' Jaguar XJR9
C.391 Ferrari GTO
C.392 Mini Metro 6R4 BP
C.393 Mini Cooper Motorworld
C.402 OMRON Porsche 962
C.406 BMW M3 Mobil
C.409 BMW M3 Demon Tweeks
C.411 Lamborghini Diablo red
C.423 Ford RS Cosworth Fina
C.424 Ford Cosworth Mondeo
C.427 Porsche 911 red
C.428 Porsche 911 black
C.430 Team Omega Securicor
C.436 Autoglass Porsche 962
C.442 Team Pirelli
C.443 Jaguar XJR9
C.444 Porsche 962C
C.445 AEG Sauber Mercedes
C.447 Pennzoil 500
C.449 Porsche 959
C.450 Ferrari F40 End
C.451 Lamborghini Diablo

C.452 Lamborghini Diablo with
  spoiler
C.453 Team Dodger
C.455 Ford RS Cosworth Texaco
C.456 Ford RS Cosworth Firestone
C.459 Shell Datsun 260Z
C.460 STP Ford Escort XR3i
C.462 BMW 318i Westminster
C.464 BMW M3
C.467 Ford Tyrrell 018
C.470 Uniroyal Ford XR2i
C.471 Ford Escort 'Barry Squibb'
C.480 Mini Metro 6R4 ESSO
C.483 Jaguar XJ220C Endurance
C.485 Delara F1

1995

C.137 Police car
C.194 Team 'Duracell'
C.197 Alfa Romeo 155
C.204 Ford Escort Cosworth
  Panasonic
C.227 Williams Renault FW15C
C.228 Team Qudos
C.229 Team Kötzting Systems
C.230 Jaguar XJ220
C.237 Ford Benetton B193
C.311 Team Texaco
C.324 Ford Escort Cosworth
C.350 F1 Goldstar
C.351 F1 Exchange Services
C.394 Porsche 911 Demon Tweeks
C.399 Mini blue
C.402 Porsche 962C Omron
C.403 Ford Escort Cosworth Hendy
C.410 Ferrari 643
C.412 Ferrari F40

Right Police Sierra XR4X4

C.416 Ford XR2i Repsol
C.417 Mini Cooper Pirelli
C.424 Ford Cosworth Mondeo
  Ford Sport
C.430 Team Omega Securicor
C.442 Team Pirelli
C.445 Sauber Mercedes AEG
C.447 Team Pennzoil
C.450 Ferrari F40
C.451 Lamborghini Diablo Racing
C.452 Lamborghini Diablo spoiler
C.453 Team Dodgers
C.462 BMW 318i Westminster
C.470 Ford XR2i Uniroyal
C.471 Ford Escort Cosworth 'Barry
  Squibb'
C.478 Mini Cooper Mobil
C.479 Formula X BP
C.480 Mini Metro 6R4 ESSO
C.483 Jaguar XJ220C Endurance
C.485 Delara F1
C.487 Formula X Firehawk
C.579 Ford Mondeo Dagenham
  Motors
C.630 Team 'Eurosport'

1996

C.137 Police car
C.194 Team Duracell
C.197 Alfa Romeo 155
C.227 Williams Renault FW15C
  No.2
C.228 Team Qudos
C.229 Team Kötzting Systems
C.230 Jaguar XJ220 Burgundy
C.251 BMW 318i Esso Ultron

C.324 Ford Escort Shell Helix

C.394 Porsche 911 Demon Tweeks

C.403 Ford Escort Hendy

C.410 Ferrari 643

C.412 Ferrari F40 Endurance
  Maxell

C.413 Porsche 911 Pirelli

C.417 Mini Cooper Pirelli

C.424 Ford Mondeo Ford Sport

C.451 Lamborghini Diablo racing red

C.452 Lamborghini Diablo with
  spoiler

C.462 BMW 318i

C.478 Mini Cooper Mobil

C.483 Jaguar XJ220C Endurance

C.522 Team Rahal Hogan

C.534 Team Pennzoil

C.536 Alfa Romeo 155 Old Spice

C.571 BMW 318i Autosport

C.572 Alfa Romeo 155 Racing

C.579 Ford Mondeo Dagenham
  Motors

C.582 Lamborghini Diablo racing
  blue

C.583 Benetton Renault B193

C.584 Williams Renault FW15C
  No.6

C.585 McLaren Mercedes MP4/10

C.587 BMW 318i Benzini

C.589 Ferrari F40 Endurance Golf

C.590 Ferrari F40 Endurance
  Kenwood

C.591 Jaguar XJ220 PC
  Automotive

C.592 Ford Escort Cepsa

C.601 AMG Mercedes C-class

C.613 Team Navico

C.616 Team Simpson

C.630 Team Eurosport

C.631 Opel Calibra V6

C.632 Vauxhall Calibra Team Joest

C.699 AMG Mercedes C-class
  Promarkt

C.716 Ford Mondeo

C.746 Ford Mondeo

C.782 Team Kwik-Fit

C.783 Team Sparco

1997

C.136 Renault Laguna 1996 Livery

C.137 Police car

C.194 Team Duracell Indy racer

C.197 Alfa Romeo 155

C.227 Williams Renault FW15C

C.230 Jaguar XJ220 Burgundy

C.324 Ford Escort Shell Helix

C.370 Ford Escort Pilot

C.394 Porsche 911 Demon Tweeks

C.412 Ferrari F40 Endurance
  Maxell

C.445 Sauber Mercedes AEG

C.483 Jaguar XJ220 Endurance

C.522 Team Rahal Hogan Indy
  racer

C.534 Team Pennzoil Indy racer

C.536 Alfa Romeo 155 Old Spice

C.559 Porsche 962C red

C.560 Porsche 911C silver

C.571 BMW 318i Autosport

C.572 Alfa Romeo 155 Racing

C.582 Lamborghini Diablo racing
  blue

C.583 Benetton Renault B193

C.585 McLaren Mercedes MP4/10
  No. 7

C.587 BMW 318i Benzina

C.589 Ferrari F40 Endurance Gulf

C.590 Ferrari F40 Endurance
  Kenwood

C.591 Jaguar XJ220C PC
  Automotive

C.592 Ford Escort Cepsa

C.601 AMG Mercedes C-class
  Sonax

C.613 Team Navico Single-seat
  racer

C.616 Team Simpson Single-seat
  racer

C.631 Opel Calibra V6 Joest Cliff

C.632 Vauxhall Calibra V6 Team
  Joest

C.699 AMG Mercedes C-class
  ProMarkt

C.701 Calibra Team Joest

C.716 Ford Mondeo 100+

C.746 Ford Mondeo Valvoline

C.782 Team Kwik-Fit Single-seat
  racer

C.783 Team Sparco Single-seat
  racer

C.2003 Lamborghini Diablo

C.2004 McLaren Mercedes
  MP4/10 No. 8

C.2005 Renault Laguna 1995
  Livery

C.2011 Ferrari 643

C.2013 Jaguar XJ220 Italian GT
  Cup

C.2014 Team Recaro Single-seat
  racer

C.2015 Team QXR Duckhams
  Single-seat racer

C.2018 Team GQ Single-seat racer

C.2027 Ford Escort Motorsport

C.2028 Ford Escort Repsol Carlos
  Sainz

C.2030 Calibra Team Rosberg

C.2031 Calibra ProMarkt

C.2032 D2 Mercedes C-class

C.2033 Mercedes C-class Team
  Persson

1998

C.136 Renault Laguna 1996
  Williams

C.137 Police car

C.227 Williams Renault FW15C
  No. 2

C.412 Ferrari F40 Endurance
  Maxell

C.483 Jaguar XJ220C Endurance
  Unipart

C.559 Porsche 962C Syntron-X

C.560 Porsche 962C Texaco

C.583 Benetton Renault B193 No. 2

C.585 McLaren Mercedes MP4/10
  No. 7

C.589 Ferrari F40 Endurance Gulf

C.591 Jaguar XJ220C Endurance
  PC Automotive

C.746 Ford Mondeo Valvoline

C.2000 Opel Vectra ProMarkt

C.2001 Vauxhall Vectra Vauxhall

C.2002 Audi A4 '96 BTCC
  Championship Winning Livery

C.2003 Lamborghini Diablo Ceric

C.2004 McLaren Mercedes
  MP4/10 No. 8

C.2005 Renault Laguna 1995
  Williams

C.2008 Audi A4 ADAC

C.2010 Renault Mégane red

C.2011 Ferrari 643 No. 1

C.2012 Williams Renault FW15C
  No. 1

C.2013 Jaguar XJ220 Italian GT
  Cup

C.2014 Team Recaro

C.2015 Team QXR Duckhams

C.2016 Team Virgin

C.2018 Team GQ

C.2027 Ford Escort Motorsport

C.2028 Ford Escort Repsol

C.2029 Renault Mégane Renault
  UK

C.2030 Opel Calibra Team Rosberg

C.2031 Opel Calibra ProMarkt

C.2032 Mercedes C-class D2

C.2033 Mercedes C-class Team
  Persson

C.2036 Ferrari F40 IGOL

C.2072 Mercedes C-Class Daim

C.2073 Opel Calibra Opel Line

C.2074 Team Texaco

C.2075 Team Kwik-Fit

C.2076 Ford Escort BP

C.2078 Renault Laguna 1997
  Williams

C.2079 Jordan Peugeot 197 No. 11

C.2080 Jordan Peugeot 197 No. 12

C.2083 Jaguar XJ220 Gold Livery

C.2084 Vauxhall Vectra Master Fit

C.2085 Opel Vectra Opel Motor
  Sport

C.2086 Audi A4 Orix

C.2087 Audi A4 Talkline

C.2088 Renault Mégane Cup
  Super

C.2089 Porsche 911 GT1 Konrad
  Motorsport

C.2090 Ford Mondeo Shell

C.2091 BMW 320i Teleshop

C.2092 Porsche 911 GT1 BMS
Scuderia Italia

C.2093 Lamborghini Diablo Teng
Tools

C.2094 Renault Mégane Diac No. 7

C.2103 Red Mini

C.2104 Yellow Mini

C.2114 Benetton Renault B193

C.2115 Ferrari 643 No. 6 1997

C.2120 Police car

C.2121 Police car

C.2124 McLaren Mercedes MP4/10
1997

1999

C.483 Jaguar XJ220 Endurance
Unipart

C.585 McClaren Mercedes MP4/10
No. 7

C.589 Ferrari F40 Endurance Gulf

C.613 Team Navico

C.2000 Opel Vectra ProMarkt

C.2003 Lamborghini Diablo

C.2004 McClaren Mercedes
MP4/10 No. 8

C.2005 Renault Laguna 1995
Williams

C.2016 Team Virgin

C.2018 Team GQ

C.2027 Ford Escort Motorsport

C.2028 Ford Escort Repsol

C.2031 Opel Calibra PromMarkt

C.2033 Mercedes C-class Team
Persson

C.2036 Ferrari F40 IGOL

C.2073 Opel Calibra Opel Line

C.2074 Team Texaco

C.2075 Team Kwik-Fit

C.2081 Mercedes CLK LM Works
No. 1

C.2082 Mercedes CLK LM Works
No. 2

C.2084 Vauxhall Vectra Master Fit

C.2085 Opel Vectra Opel Motor
Sport

C.2086 Audi A4 Orix

C.2087 Audi A4 Talkline

C.2088 Renault Mégane Cup
Super

C.2091 BMW 320i Teleshop

C.2092 Porsche 911 GTI

C.2095 Team Bridgestone

C.2096 Team Minolta

C.2103 Red Mini

C.2104 Yellow Mini

C.2105 McLaren Mercedes 1997
No. 9

C.2107 Audi A4 BTCC No. 1

C.2113 Team Avon Tyres

C.2114 Benetton Renault 1997 No. 7

C.2115 Ferrari 643 1997 No. 6

C.2118 Subaru Impreza WRC
Works

C.2119 Toyota Corolla WRC Works

C.2120 Police car

C.2121 Police car

C.2124 McLaren Mercedes MP4/10
1997 No. 10

C.2126 Jordan Mugen Honda No. 9

C.2127 Jordan Mugen Honda No. 10

C.2161 Williams FW20 No. 1

C.2162 Williams FW20 No. 2

C.2163 Audi A4 Engen

C.2165 Opel Vectra TNT

C.2166 Renault Laguna Nescafé
Blend 37

C.2167 Renault Laguna DC Cook

C.2168 BMW Castrol

C.2169 BMW Fina

C.2170 Ford Mondeo Works Team

C.2171 Ford Escort Works No. 7

C.2174 Ford Escort Works No. 8

C.2177 Subaru Impreza Stomil

C.2178 Toyota Corolla WRC

C.2179 Williams FW20 1999 No.5

C.2180 Williams FW20 1999 No. 6

C.2187 Benetton B193/99 No. 10

C.2190 Porsche 911 GTI IBM

C.2191 Porsche 911 GTI Playstation

C.2192 Lamborghini Diablo
Valvoline

C.2193 Lamborghini Diablo SV

C.2194 TVR Speed 12 Road Trim

C.2195 TVR Speed 12 Race Trim

C.2200 Lotus 7 Classic

C.2201 Caterham
17 No. 27

C.2202 Porsche 911
1GTI 100+

C.2229 Porsche 911 GTI
1Paragon

C.2230 Lotus 7 Classic

C.2231 Caterham 7 No. 28

2000 Issue 1

C.2081 Mercedes CLK GT1 No. 1

C.2082 Mercedes CLK GT1 No. 2

C.2095 Team Bridgestone No. 7

C.2096 Team Minolta No. 8

C.2107 Audi A4 BTCC No. 1

C.2112 Team Agip No. 10

C.2113 Team Avon Tyres No. 9

C.2115 Ferrari 643 No. 6

C.2118 Subaru Impreza WRC1
Works No. 3

C.2119 Toyota Corolla WRC No. 5

C.2120 Police car

C.2121 Police car

C.2126 Jordan Mugan Honda
No. 9

C.2127 Jordan Mugan Honda
No.10

C.2131 Audi A4 Euro Jever No. 14

C.2143 No. 12 Mobil 1 Ford Taurus

C.2144 Vauxhall Vectra Works STW
No. 3

C.2145 Renault Laguna Nescafé
Blend 37 No. 5

C.2161 Williams Mécachrome
FW20 No. 1

C.2162 Williams Mécachrome
FW20 No. 2

C.2167 Renault Laguna DC Cook
No. 21

C.2172 Ford Mondeo Works No. 4

C.2173 Toyota Corolla Works 1999
No. 3

C.2184 Toyota Corolla Privateer
1999

C.2187 Benetton Renault B193
1999 No. 10

C.2188 Porsche 911 GT1 Team
Champion No. 38

Above Porsche 962C

C.2189 TVR Speed 12 ESSO Ultron
No. 42

C.2190 Porsche 911 GT1 IBM No. 26

C.2194 TVR Speed 12 Road Trim

C.2195 TVR Speed 12 Works No. 12

C.2200 Lotus 7 Classic

C.2201 Caterham 7 No. 27

C.2208 Rusty Wallace No. 2 Ford
Taurus

C.2209 TVR Speed 12 Demon
Tweeks No. 18

C.2214 VW Beetle Cabriolet

C.2215 VW Beetle Cabriolet

C.2217 Exide Batteries No. 99 Ford
Taurus

C.2218 McDonald's No. 94 Ford
Taurus

C.2219 Valvoline No. 6 Ford Taurus

C.2225 John Deere No. 97 Ford
Taurus

C.2229 Porsche 911 GT1 Paragon
No. 2

C.2230 Lotus 7 Classic

C.2231 Caterham 7 No. 28

C.2233 VW Beetle Pirelli No. 3

C.2234 VW Beetle Movil 1 No. 14

C.2255 Subaru Impreza Works
1999 No. 6

C.2256 Subaru Impreza Belgacom
1999 No. 16

C.2260 McLaren Mercedes No. 1

C.2261 McLaren Mercedes No. 2

C.2269 Lotus Racing No. 5

C.2270 Lotus 7 Racing No. 8

C.2271 Caterham 7 Road Trim

C.2272 Caterham 7 Road Trim

C.2273 Police car

C.2303 Vauxhall Vectra Masterfit No. 8

2000 Issue 2

C.2081 Mercedes CLK GT1 No. 1

C.2082 Mercedes CLK GT1 No. 2

C.2095 Team Bridgestone No. 7

C.2096 Team Minolta No. 8

C.2107 Audi A4 BTCC No. 1

C.2112 Team Agip No. 10

C.2115 Ferrari 643 No. 6

C.2118 Subaru Impreza WRC Works No.3

C.2120 Police car

C.2121 Police car

C.2131 Audi A4 Eurp Jever No. 14

C.2144 Opel Vectra STW No. 3

C.2145 Renault Laguna Nescafé Blend 37 No. 5

C.2188 Porsche 911 GT1 Team Champion No. 38

C.2189 TVR Speed 12 ESSO Ultron No. 42

C.2126 Jordan Mugan Honda No. 9

C.2127 Jordan Mugan Honda No. 10

C.2161 Williams Mécachrome FW20 No. 1

C.2162 Williams Mécachrome FW20 No. 2

C.2172 Ford Mondeo BTCC 1999 No. 4

C.2173 Toyota Corolla Works 1999 No. 3

C.2175 Ford Focus WRC Iridium No. 1

C.2176 Ford Focus WRC Works McRae 2000 No5

C.2183 Toyota Corolla V Rally

C.2184 Toyota Corolla Privateer 1999 No. 24

C.2187 Benetton Renault B193 1999 No. 10

C.2190 Porsche 911 GT1 IBM No. 26

C.2200 Lotus 7 Classic

C.2201 Caterham 7 No. 27

C.2208 Rusty Wallace No. 2 Ford Taurus

C.2209 TVR Speed 12 Demon Tweeks No. 18

C.2217 Exide Batteries No. 99 Ford Taurus

C.2218 McDonald's No. 94 Ford Taurus

C.2219 Valvoline No. 6 Ford Taurus

C.2225 John Deere No. 97 Ford Taurus

C.2231 Caterham 7 No. 28

C.2233 VW Beetle Pirelli No. 3

C.2234 VW Beetle Mobil No. 14

C.2255 Subaru Impreza Works 1999 No. 6

C.2256 Subaru Impreza Belgacom 1999 No. 16

C.2257 Subaru Impreza Works 2000 No.3 Burns

C.2258 Cadillac Northstar Le Mans Prototype GM Racing No. 1

C.2259 Cadillac Northstar Le Mans Prototype Dams No. 3

C.2260 McLaren Mercedes No. 1

C.2261 McLaren Mercedes No. 2

C.2264 Williams BMW No. 9

C.2265 Williams BMW No. 10

C.2266 Benetton Renault B193 2000 No. 11

C.2269 Lotus 7 Racing No. 5

C.2270 Lotus 7 Racing No. 8

C.2271 Caterham 7 Road Trim

C.2272 Caterham 7 Road Trim

C.2273 Police car

C.2279 Mobil 1 No. 12 Ford Taurus 2000

C.2280 DeWalt No. 17 Ford Taurus

C.2281 Exide Batteries No. 99 Ford Taurus 2000

C.2283 Valvoline No. 6 Ford Taurus 2000

C.2284 Lycos.com Pontiac Grand Prix

C.2303 Vauxhall Vectra Masterfit No. 8

C.2309 Vauxhall Vectra BTCC 2000 No. 5

C.2310 Opel Vectra

C.2311 Ford Mondeo BTCC 2000 No. 3

C.2312 Toyota Corolla WRC Zucchetti

C.2313 Subaru Impreza Norisbank No. 30

C.2314 VW Beetle Cabriolet

C.2315 VW Beetle Cabriolet

2001

C.2018 Team GQ No. 18

C.2081 Mercedes CLK GT1 No. 1

C.2082 Mercedes CLK GT1 No. 2

C.2096 Team Minolta No. 8

C.2112 Team Agip No. 10

C.2115 Ferrari 643 No. 6

C.2126 Jordan Mugan Honda No. 9

C.2172 Ford Mondeo Works Rapid Fit 1999 No. 4

C.2175 Ford Focus WRC Iridium Privateer No. 1

C.2176 Ford Focus WRC Works McRae 2000 No.5

C.2183 Toyota Corolla V Rally No. 45

C.2184 Toyota Corolla Privateer 1999 No. 24

C.2187 Benetton Renault B193 1999 No. 10

C.2189 TVR Speed 12 Ultron No. 42

C.2200 Lotus 7 Classic

C.2209 TVR Speed 12 Demon Tweeks No. 18

C.2231 Caterham 7 Comma No. 28

C.2257 Subaru Impreza Works 2000 No. 3 Burns

C.2258 Cadillac Northstar Le Mans GM Racing No. 1

C.2259 Cadillac Northstar Le Mans Dams No. 3

C.2260 McLaren Mercedes No. 1

C.2261 Mc Laren Mercedes No. 2

C.2264 Williams BMW No. 9

C.2265 Williams BMW No. 10

C.2266 Benetton Renault 2000

C.2269 Lotus 7 Racing No. 5

C.2270 Lotus 7 Racing No. 8

C.2271 Caterham 7 Road Trim

C.2272 Caterham 7 Road Trim

C.2273 Police car

C.2274 Porsche 911 GT3R Paragon

C.2275 Porsche 911 GT3R Red Bull

C.2278 TVR Speed 12 Scania Works 2000 No. 27

C.2279 Mobil 1 No. 12 Ford Taurus

C.2280 De Walt No. 17 Ford Taurus

C.2281 Exide Batteries No. 99 Ford Taurus

C.2283 Valvoline No. 6 Ford Taurus

C.2286 Tide No. 32 Ford Taurus

C.2297 Opel V8 Coupé DTM

C.2298 Opel V8 Coupé DTM

C.2303 Vauxhall Vectra Works Masterfit No. 8

C.2309 Vauxhall Vectra Works Masterfit 2000 No. 5

C.2310 Opel Vectra Opel Line No. 20

C.2311 Ford Mondeo Works Rapid Fit 2000 No. 3

C.2312 Toyota Corolla WRC Zucchetti No. 18

C.2313 Subaru Impreza Norisbank No. 30

C.2314 Beetle Cabriolet

C.2315 VW Beetle Cabriolet

C.2336 VW Beetle 2000 No. 11

C.2337 VW Beetle 2000 No. 12

C.2343 Ford Focus Laukkanen No. 19

C.2344 Caterham 7 Peter Ritchie Racing

C.2345 Caterham 7 Team Taran

Index of Cars

Picture Credits

Unless otherwise stated, all model and accessory photography by Gary Ombler, using the collection of Chris Gregory.

All drawings from the catalogue collection of Chris Gregory and reproduced by kind permission of Scalextric.

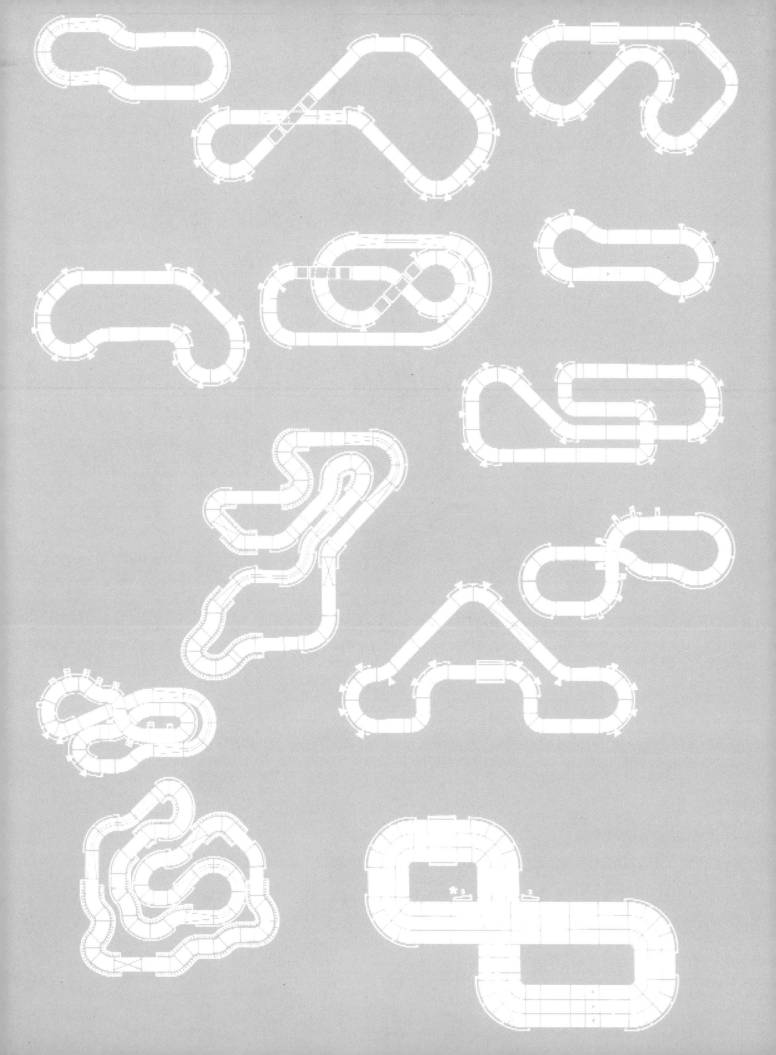